Junk Tech

Series « Antidoxa »,
directed by Xavier Desmaison

First published in French under the title:
Junk Tech. Comment la Silicon Valley a gagné la guerre du marketing
© 2020, Hermann Éditeurs
All rights reserved

Cover Illustrations:
Frites dans une enveloppe de papier © Zoran Mladenovic/123rf
Premium mobile phone screen © rawpixel/123rf

www.editions-hermann.fr

ISBN : 979 1 0370 1534 1

© 2021, Hermann Éditeurs, 6 rue Labrouste, 75015 Paris.

Jean-Marc Bally   Xavier Desmaison

JUNK TECH

HOW SILICON VALLEY WON THE MARKETING WAR

Depuis 1876

Introduction

Very Bad Trip

A wake-up call for France and Europe in a digital civilization

> "Europeans just react to events as they happen and hope things don't get worse. The indefinite pessimist can't know whether the inevitable decline will be fast or slow, catastrophic or gradual. All he can do is wait for it to happen, so he might as well eat, drink, and be merry in the meantime: hence Europe's famous vacation mania."
>
> Peter Thiel,
> *Zero to One: Notes on Startups,*
> *or How to Build the Future*

Criticizing the French and Europeans for their technological backwardness has pretty much become a cliché. Outperformed not only by Silicon Valley but also by China, the "Old Continent" is making a seemingly unimpressive début in the fourth industrial revolution. Incapable of developing the equivalent of GAFA, NATU or BATX[1], Europe's nations

---

1. GAFA is the acronym for the American "Big Four," Google, Amazon, Facebook, Apple; NATU stands for the four companies known for digital "disruption" Netflix, Airbnb, Tesla, Uber; and BATX for the four Chinese tech giants Baidu, Alibaba, Tencent, Xiaomi.

and companies are said to be losing the battle for innovation. Limited by a fragmented market and insufficient funding, lacking the means to compete on a level playing field… a list of their shortcomings could fill a book.

Although these arguments are not all unfounded, many critics are gravely misreading the myths and rhetoric of the entrepreneurs from the San Francisco Bay Area. If we are to believe California's "techno-magicians," Silicon Valley has a substantial lead over the rest of the world. Thanks to their expertise in digital technology, algorithms, big data and artificial intelligence, its tech companies are said to be developing solutions that would eventually solve all of humanity's ills. As a result of their ultra-creative minds and to "fledgling sta tups breastfed on a cornucopia of venture capital[2]," they are credited with an outpouring of revolutionary inventions and discoveries. In short, Silicon Valley's technological solutionism is portrayed as the key to the future.

But in our view, this way of thinking has more to do with storytelling than with reality. Worse still, this belief in California's technological superiority is preventing France and Europe from making the right choices, choices that would allow them to make up for their slow start and compete on a global scale. In the race for innovation, French authorities and French companies are forgetting a crucial ingredient— marketing—which they mistakenly reduce to an operational function when in reality it plays an important role in essential strategies.

This intuition, which we have shared for several years, was confirmed by the Covid-19 pandemic, a crisis that brought together two contradictory dynamics. On the one hand, technological platforms such as Amazon, Netflix or Zoom showed that their model is valid; their business was boosted by the pandemic in that they seemed to respond efficiently

---

2. Philippe Laurier, "La Silicon Valley et le mythe de la génération spontanée," *Latribune.fr*, February 17, 2019.

to a certain number of the expectations of today's connected consumers. On the other hand, the situation also showed the real incapacity of Silicon Valley and Economy 2.0's leaders in dealing with concrete problems related to the safety, health or industrial production of our societies. As Marc Andreessen—a tech guru and entrepreneur who until now was a champion of the dematerialized and software-dominated world—says, the pandemic highlighted the limits of an innovation ecosystem and "our widespread inability to 'build.'" At a time when people and institutions were urgently in need of masks, medical therapies and ventilators, what did these companies actually contribute[3]?

This question is one of many that inspired our thinking and our conversations in writing this book. What if Silicon Valley's technological supremacy were just a mirage? What if its real strength lies less in its technical prowess than in its marketing culture? What if France and Europe, by following this model without questioning the real causes of its successes (and failures), has been going down the wrong path? What if the prophets of Silicon Valley were above all brilliant communication strategists, dream peddlers who have perfectly mastered the art of storytelling and know just how to take advantage of consumers' fundamental aspirations? What if this crisis we have been dealing with since early 2020 were also providing us with an incredible opportunity to go back to square one?

Over time, our responses to these questions began to feel more and more self-evident: given their technological and human capital, there is no reason for France and Europe to be so far behind Silicon Valley and China. In barely thirty years, we have gone from being America's rival in the battle for digital supremacy to being the underdog—as if after a night

---

3. Marc Andreessen, "It's time to build," *a16z.com*, April 18, 2020; David Rotman, "Covid-19 has blown apart the myth of Silicon Valley innovation," *www.technologyreview.com*, April 25, 2020.

of celebrating our past successes, we had woken up in a world whose logic and codes we could no longer understand.

In France's case, this situation seems totally unnatural. Undermined by rhetoric that is defeatist and declinist, we have resigned ourselves to the idea that our country is lagging behind in new technologies as if it were a foregone conclusion, set in stone, but upon closer inspection, it looks more like an anomaly. If we look at the history of innovation in the twentieth century, we can clearly see that the French have a long history as pioneers.

A Frenchman, Georges Doriot (1899-1987), launched the first venture capital company in the United States in the 1950s and contributed to the development of the startup economy[4]. The French also made an enormous investment in developing disruptive technology innovations, creating companies in such diversified sectors as energy (nuclear power), aeronautics (the Concorde), railways (the high-speed train), telecommunications (the Minitel, Alcatel, the Global System for Mobile Communications or GSM standard[5]) and micro-processors (the smart card). By way of the European Council for Nuclear Research (CERN), the French were also involved in the emergence of the Web[6]. Until the mid-1990s, a number

---

4. "Hailed in1999 by *The Wall Street Journal* as one of ten people in the twentieth century who had the greatest influence on entrepreneurship, Georges Doriot also left behind a double legacy in his native France. In 1930, he helped the Paris Chamber of Commerce and Industry create the Centre de perfectionnement aux affaires (now part of the HEC group). And in 1957, he contributed to the birth of Insead in Fontainebleau." Claude Barjonet, "Georges Doriot, inventeur du capital-risque," *Lesechos. fr*, July 8, 2014.

5. The Centre national d'études des télécommunications (le CNET, the forerunner of Orange Labs), the *Deutsche Bundespost* and Scandinavian operators played a leading role in the development of this standard, which has become a worldwide standard to the detriment of American standards.

6. The World Wide Web was created in the late 1980s and early 1990s by two European engineers and computer scientists, Tim Berners-Lee of Britain and Robert Cailliau of Belgium, at CERN in Geneva.

of French companies were national champions poised for digital transformation, not to mention that with their appetite for innovation, the French had always been considered early adopters of digital technology.

But then the engine stalled. The French did not evolve at the same pace as the U.S. during the first wave of the Internet, search engines and social networks. For example, Viadeo, a French business network, and Dailymotion, a French video-sharing technology platform, both pioneers, never really developed in comparison with LinkedIn and YouTube. As for the French unicorns BlaBlaCar (a carpooling service), Deezer (an online music streaming platform) and Doctolib (a telehealth provider), they are still struggling in their efforts to go global and achieve the same results as their Californian counterparts, although rare exceptions such as Criteo (an online advertising platform) confirm the influence of French tech outside our borders.

This harsh disparity seems all the more incomprehensible in that the French have powerful advantages—talented engineers and developers seamlessly established in Silicon Valley; a pool of startups; a new generation of entrepreneurs helping to renew business models; government support for the digital economy; the remarkable growth of private equity in an ecosystem that is increasingly attracting foreign capital[7]; and the synergy of large companies working with startups to strengthen their innovation culture. As a result, there is more reason for hope than for dismay.

Even so, the situation remains a mystery. Why, despite of all its assets, is it so difficult for the French to shift gears? Even if the conditions for the innovation ecosystem in France and in Europe are less favorable than in California, why are they lagging so far behind in the digital revolution?

We believe that the reason is less technological than cultural. France and Europe have not managed to transpose to the digital

---

7. *Businessfrance.fr*, April 24, 2019, "Le capital-investissement français bat de nouveaux records."

economy their principal added value in such sectors as the service industry or luxury goods. They have not appealed to something emotional and irrational that resonates with peoples' dreams and desires; they have not generated "dependency phenomena[8]" to keep customers coming back to their products and services, nor have they defined a sense of purpose that resonates with deep-rooted individual and collective ambitions.

In contrast, the Silicon Valley entrepreneurs, having observed the transition from a consumer society to the aspirational age, invented a new type of merchandise to cultivate product addiction and mass narcissism, not unlike junk food— we call it "*junk tech.*" *Junk tech* is a magical combination of the talent to tap into the cultural zeitgeist, the ability to build a coherent offering and the power to shape narratives that embrace people's individual and collective desires. It puts consumers under a spell, like a love potion[9].

Convinced that "tech" is the crucial factor in the equation, too many French and European decision-makers—whether business executives or investors—are fighting the wrong battle. They have fallen victim to the mirage of Silicon Valley and the adverse effects of the technocentric approach, and are trying to reproduce California's winning recipe but without the right ingredients.

Going viral has become one of the trademarks of our time. The Covid-19 pandemic is only one symptom among so

---

8. Benoît Heilbrunn, *Market Mediations: Semiotic Investigations on Consumers, Objects and Brands,* Palgrave Macmillan, May 2015.

9. "And if the brand finally played the role of what in ancient times and the Middle Ages was called a love potion? [...] Does not marketing ultimately aim to put the consumer under its spell [...]? The brand may be understood by analogy as a kind of pharmakon that wants a consumer to become permanently attached [...] In Greek, pharmakon defines any substance, regardless of whether it is beneficial or harmful. A pharmakon is both cure and poison, and by extension any act that preserves, ensures salvation, improves one's condition, as well as any act that poisons and corrupts." *Ibid.*

many of the laws according to which today's world operates. The continuous media uproar, the 'infodemic' (a surplus of information and misinformation), the endless trends and the adoption of new consumerist habits are developing exponentially and at breakneck speed. Differentiating between underlying trends and an epiphenomenon is becoming less and less easy. Whether we are consumers, investors, communicators, managers of a large corporation or a startup, we are all are finding it increasingly difficult to find our way.

The goal of this book is neither to celebrate the successes of the Californian startups nor to cynically glorify the triumph of addiction marketing, but rather to dispel a number of illusions and misunderstandings about the mechanisms of innovation in the *junk tech* era. We are convinced that French and European companies can shine in the digital galaxy if they focus more on the fundamentals of marketing and apply this philosophy to the major challenges that are emerging in the wake of the fourth industrial revolution: energy transition, biotechnologies and health, responses to the climate emergency, infrastructures and the Internet of things, smart cities, hardware and deep tech. All of these are areas in which we must break new ground and whenever possible, alongside technological imperatives, lay the foundations for sustainable business models and innovations that are virtuous and respond to the aspirations of today's citizen-consumers. The Covid-19 pandemic has shown that there are still many unexplored areas for improving the future of our societies, for embracing industry 4.0 and for putting it to work so that Europe can play a leading role in the digital age.

I.

TECHNOLOGY MIRAGES AND MARKETING MIRACLES: THE ORIGINS OF *JUNK TECH*

"Too many once great American firms have become complacent, careless, and out of touch. They pursue short-term, bottom-line targets and bury themselves in technical or financial intricacies, while they neglect the substance—the products and the customers—of their business."

DANNY MILLER,
The Icarus Paradox: How Exceptional Companies Bring about Their Own Downfall

In 2015, Jeff Immelt had just completed General Electric's acquisition of Alstom's power and grid businesses, and the international press was full of praise for his strategic leadership skills. Supported by his peers and by the Obama administration, Immelt, successor to the legendary Jack Welch, was viewed as one of the planet's most powerful and inspired leaders. Propelled to the position of GE's chief executive officer just a few days before the September 11 tragedy in 2001, had succeeded in consolidating the company's position in spite of the bleak economic context. He had weathered the financial storm of 2008, refocused the group on industrial activities and promised to transform the conglomerate into a software company. Immelt's decisions and intuition were unanimously celebrated, so much so that many predicted he was destined for a brilliant political career. Everything seemed to be going according to plan for this fan of Ronald Reagan and the TV series *The West Wing*[1]. But two years later, GE experienced an unprecedented decrease in market capitalization, and Jeff Immelt soon epitomized the fallen industrial giant. Forced to step down as president after sixteen years, he lost his status as a leader admired by the media and the political microcosm, and his supposed future in Washington, D.C., became irrelevant…

Our goal is not to attack GE's former CEO. Like so many others before him, Jeff Immelt made a series of decisions that led his company to disaster, and those who replaced him cannot boast of achieving better results… Management guides are full of stories about companies and leaders who brush up against the stars and then burn their wings; unfortunately, this is a common scenario. It repeats itself every time organizations become ideologically rigid, close themselves off and distance themselves from their main objective. When companies "stop making the right stuff for the right markets [they] pay the price: earnings plummet, stock prices collapse, and managers are dismissed[2]." Think about, for instance, the symbolic paths of Nokia, Kodak or Blackberry. Everyone believed these companies were invincible, but when they failed to anticipate trends and grasp their customers' underlying needs and expectations, they fell at an impressive speed, despite their technological superiority.

---

1. Thuy-Diep Nguyen, "Qui est Jeff Immelt, le patron de General Electric qui veut racheter Alstom?" *Challenges.fr*, April 30, 2014.

2. Danny Miller, *The Icarus Paradox: How Exceptional Companies Bring about Their Own Downfall: New Lessons in the Dynamics of Corporate Success, Decline, and Renewal. Harper Business,* January 1990.

This phenomenon is expected to increase sharply in the coming years: all the companies that neglect the market and instead take a technocentric approach will be doomed decline or disappear. From the consumer society to the aspirational age[3], we have shifted to a world in which commercial awareness and marketing skills are more important than technological firepower. Too intelligent to accept this simple principle, many leaders are guiding their organizations into a dead end[4].

1. GENERAL ELECTRIC'S TWOFOLD MISTAKE

What is interesting about GE is that its downfall perfectly illustrates these mistakes—a lack of foresight on the part of its leaders regarding the profound evolution of their own markets, and a disproportionate belief in the transformative power of the digital revolution.

Lack of foresight in market development

First, GE's management believed that yesterday's achievements would be tomorrow's successes, a belief that led to its acquisition of Alstom's power and grid businesses and the merger of GE Oil and Gas with Baker Hughes. GE invested colossal sums of money in order to strengthen its grip on the fossil fuel sector and increase the results produced by the oligopoly. The purchase of Alstom Power, which exceeded $10 billion, was one of the conglomerate's most expensive acquisitions. And it was made at the worst of times, when renewable energy sources, starting with solar photovoltaics, were becoming more competitive and were starting to have greater impact on the energy sector by becoming credible

---

3. For more information on this, see Chapter III.
4. For more information on this, see Chapter V.

alternatives. Although GE forecast an increase in demand associated with gas-fired power plants, quite the opposite occurred; rather than rising, GE Power's profits fell by 45 percent[5]. Obsessed with the development of activities they considered profitable, Jeff Immelt and his board of directors failed to identify the great changes facing customers due to the rapid rise of renewable energy. The "Icarus paradox," a dynamic described by Danny Miller, a Canadian economist, is an apt description of this error, which often appears during industrial disasters. As the company continued to grow without taking the overall environment into account, it made poor investments and became oblivious to what was essential: the importance of its value proposition.

This is a recurring problem in mergers and acquisitions (M&A). As Roger L. Martin, author of *Creating Great Choices*[6], explains, in these situations, the greatest success comes from "integrative thinking": using the tension of opposing ideas to help create transformative new answers, in order to make your products and services more appealing, indispensable and addictive. Remember when Google took over Android, and when Facebook bought Instagram? The idea of bringing them together makes so much sense that today it seems obvious. But if they are disassociated from strategic thinking about customers' expectations and the fundamental value companies can offer, these kinds of operations bring almost nothing (except for serious problems). Many large corporations have paid the price for this lack of vision: News Corp with the social networking service MySpace, Microsoft with the Nokia smartphone business, HP with

---

5. Geoff Colvin, "What the Hell Happened at GE?" *Fortune.com*, May 24, 2018.

6. Jennifer Riel, Roger L. Martin, "Creating Great Choices. A Leader's Guide to Integrative Thinking," *Harvard Business Review Press*, September 2017.

Autonomy, a software company[7]. Each of these acquisitions led to fiasco. Whether it's a question of establishing leadership in a sector or diversifying, M&A only make sense if they serve the organization's value proposition. This obvious point is sadly all too often overlooked by companies that rush into an "overexpansion" that becomes "all-consuming," to the detriment of imagination and creativity[8].

An excessive belief in the power of digital transformation

Second, Jeff Immelt gave in to the technology mirage propagated by Silicon Valley gurus and the apostles of "technological solutionism[9]." In 2015, when Immelt announced that GE would become a "top 10 software company" and capitalize on the potential of the Internet of Things, he was simply repeating the famous phrase penned a few years earlier by Marc Andreessen, an entrepreneur and investor: "Software Is Eating the World[10]." But in this instance, GE's outsized appetite was consistent with Andreessen's slogan. To a large extent, Jeff Immelt's all-consuming digital ambitions accelerated the group's downfall. The launch of Predix, an industrial software platform, and the creation of a new GE Digital business unit, both amid much publicity, did not meet the expected success. Despite the fact that 1,000 first-class engineers had been recruited in San Ramon, a stone's throw from Silicon Valley,

---

7. Roger L. Martin, "GE's Fall Has Been Accelerated by Two Problems. Most Other Big Companies Face Them, Too," *Hbr.org*, June 29, 2018.

8. "The venturing trajectory converts growth-driven, entrepreneurial Builders, companies managed by imaginative leaders and creative planning and financial staffs, into impulsive, greedy Imperialists, who severely overtax their resources by expanding helter-skelter into businesses they know nothing about." Danny Miller, *op. cit.*

9. Evgeny Morozov, *To Save Everything, Click Here. Technology, Solutionism, and the Urge to Fix Problems that Don't Exist*, Penguin, July 2014.

10. Marc Andreessen, "Why Software Is Eating the World," *The Wall Street Journal*, August 20, 2011.

the objectives set by management were never achieved: revenue barely exceeded $1 billion, whereas Jeff Immelt anticipated a profit of six times that amount by 2016, and spent at least $4 billion developing Predix. GE bet everything on technical excellence, but failed to convince customers to adopt their offer and to make it addictive.

According to several observers, the factors that explain this are more cultural than technological. The failure of Predix and GE Digital mainly reflects the difficulties organizations face in moving from a product-centric model to one that is service-oriented[11]. This is one of the specific challenges for large companies in the aspirational age. Digital transformation does not consist only of skills, resources and sophisticated innovation; more importantly, it requires a change in mindset inside the company. Billions of euros of investment, an armada of highly qualified engineers and a flashy communication campaign cannot change this fact. If an organization continues to apply the recipes of yesteryear to develop disruptive solutions, every chance exists that its innovation system will be inconsequential rather than truly effective manner.

This was the mistake made with Predix and GE Digital. When the platform found new partners, "the focus was usually on generating short-term revenue and not long-term value to GE's end customers[12]," in keeping with the traditional approach of quarterly performance tracking, a method that often proves incompatible with the emergence of creative solutions. In addition, "GE talked of making Predix a true development platform for third-party developers. But in practice almost all the software being built around Predix was from GE's own business units or paid partners[13]." In other

---

11. Ravi Kumar, "Lessons to learn from GE's IoT Platform, Predix's failure?" *Medium.com*, August 18, 2018.

12. Alex Moazed, "Why GE Digital Failed," *Inc.com*, January 8, 2018.

13. *Ibid.*

words, the company did not utilize the right ingredients for its digital transformation. It failed to solve the famous "innovator's dilemma" a concept shaped by Clayton Christensen, an academic and business consultant—to make its traditional activities flourish while relying on breakthrough innovations[14]. With less money and smaller teams that would have had more freedom in imagining services adapted to customers, the company would undoubtedly have had better results[15]. Prisoners of corporate culture and the technology mirage, GE's leaders precipitated their company's collapse. Some critics badmouthed Jeff Immelt, claiming he failed to listen to his employees and acted as if he was the smartest man in the company[16]. In any case, it is certain is that he did not heed signs of weakness in the market. This is the story's great irony: when he joined GE in 1982, he was in the marketing department.

2. Walmart's rekindled hopes

An inheritor of the consumer society

In contrast to GE, Walmart, the American retail giant, followed a very different path, making a quick turnaround after first missing out on the digital revolution. Not long ago, observers held little hope for Walmart, which had been

---

14. Clayton M. Christensen, *The Innovator's Dilemma. When New Technologies Cause Great Firms to Fail*, Harvard Business Review Press, January 2016.

15. This is actually what Jeff Bezos did with his famous "two-pizza-team rule": to facilitate innovation within a large group, you need small internal teams (a group small enough to be adequately fed with two pizzas), which allows for more thinking outside the box. This approach was used to give birth to Amazon Web Services (AWS), an entity specialized in data storage (the cloud), which becomes one of the company's main sources of profit.

16. Geoff Colvin, *op. cit.*

devastated by the explosion of e-commerce and by Amazon's incredible success. Founded in 1962, in a moment of widespread conspicuous consumption, the group had a motto that reflected its legacy, "Always low prices," which it held onto until the mid-2000s. In yesterday's world, price was the main differentiating factor for the consumer. But this is no longer the case. In the aspirational age, in which people dream not of owning things but of becoming someone, of achieving something, customers are looking for a user experience that goes beyond daily access to an inexpensive, standardized product.

In 2016, after the closure of hundreds of stores and poor performance with e-commerce, the group decided to rethink its strategy. At the time, the "sluggishness of online sales continued despite repeated efforts to reverse the trend. To take just one example, Walmart Labs, a subsidiary of Walmart dedicated to innovation based in Mountain View, California, created following the acquisition of the startup Kosmix, a specialist in search engines dedicated to e-commerce, exists since April 2011. It was clear that recurring R&D spending was not producing the expected results[17]," again demonstrating the limits of a technocentric approach. It was not enough to set up teams in Silicon Valley to conquer digital space and be innovative. The gap between Walmart's customers, mostly older people with modest income, and its website's target audience was proving difficult to bridge.

A cultural and marketing turnaround

A game changer occurred in August 2016, when Walmart acquired Jet.com, an e-commerce startup co-founded by Marc Lore, an entrepreneur who had once briefly worked at Amazon. The retailer's decision paid off, because in so doing the company called into question its way of functioning and it habitual reflexes: "Instead of 'Walmartizing'

---

17. Yves Pizay, "La transformation digitale par absorption : le cas Walmart," *Digital-happy.kea-partners.com*, March 14, 2019.

Jet, Walmart decided to become 'Jetized[18]" by cultivating "constant customer orientation[19]" and expanding beyond its traditional base thanks to the smart-card system, which lowers the price of products when you buy more.[20] The company attracted new consumers and increased market share via online sales by changing its marketing culture. Without renouncing its philosophy and its DNA as a champion of low prices, the group regained its strength by placing customer satisfaction at the heart of its value proposition. In its battle against Amazon, Walmart gradually built a mythology to help it attract new customers: "The Arkansas retailer, new hero of American commerce, driven by the awakening of deep America, became the one to devour the new economy[21]." Although far from having caught up with Jeff Bezos' company in online marketing, the company shifted from being a survivor of the old world to being a contender in the digital galaxy.

Like Accor (the French hotel group), which survived the arrival of Airbnb, or Rousselet (G7 taxis), which managed to adapt to Uber's infiltrating the market, Walmart's story proves that traditional organizations are not doomed so long as they approach digital transformation from the right angle. In order to continue selling its products or services, a company must understand that technology is only an intermediary—the key lies elsewhere, in understanding the behavior, emotions

---

18. Flore Fauconnier, "Comment Walmart se transforme à grande vitesse," *Lsa-conso.fr*, January 31, 2018.

19. Yves Pizay, *op. cit.*

20. "In keeping with the principle that *prices drop as you shop*, the unit price for each object added to the consumer's basket decreases in real time with each added product. According to a more classic procedure, the consumer also has the possibility of lowering the unit price of the products in the basket by choosing to buy the same product in bulk. The consumer can also lower the total price of the order by playing on the various available options: not to subscribe to the right of return or choose to pay by debit card are all means proposed to the customer who wants to save money." *Ibid.*

21. Flore Fauconnier, *op.cit.*

and values that drive people in the twenty-first century[22]. Moving on from "Always low prices" to write a new chapter in its history, Walmart gave itself an ideological heart (or a Big Hairy Audacious Goal[23]) that fits more closely the codes and imagination of our era: "We save people money so they can live better."

In today's age of technological proliferation, many companies believe they will improve their performance and competitiveness by accelerating their digital transformation, by surrounding themselves with outside consultants or by developing cutting-edge products. Last year, while close to $1.3 trillion was spent on digital transformation, it was estimated that $900 billion went to waste[24]. Why? Because many organizations don't change their culture, don't listen to their customers and substitute the fundamentals of strategy with a technocentric approach. At the heart of the digital civilization, superstition has taken hold, attributing an almost magical power to new technologies, disruption and digitalization. In any case, allowing $900 billion to go up in smoke is quite the magic trick…

3. "IT'S THE MARKETING, STUPID": WHEN TECHNOLOGIES' PEAK FAILS

Great innovation needs great marketing

As Denise Lee Yohn, an expert on brand leadership, aptly states, great innovation needs great marketing—the ability to maximize value creation by deciphering, anticipating and even creating markets. Far from being limited to utilitarian

---

22. For more information on this, see Chapter III.

23. For more information on this, see Chapter VI.

24. Behnam Tabrizi, Ed Lam, Kirk Girard, Vernon Irvin, "Digital Transformation Is Not About Technology," *Hbr.org*, March 13, 2019.

functions or a simple ensemble of techniques for generating and holding onto customers, great marketing is not played out through downstream tactics. The power of the marketing function comes from upstream—from creating markets, from understanding people's basic needs and motivations, from identifying customers and developing the go-to-market and usage ecosystem[25]. In most companies, the word "marketing" has such negative connotations that it would probably have to be changed in order to convince its decision-makers to go further in that direction… Try to persuade someone fresh out of business or engineering school that their company's critical success factor lies in marketing, and you will see how incongruous your comment seems to them, at best simplistic, and at worst ridiculous.

Even the most innovative companies can fall into this trap by neglecting marketing operations. This is what happened with Google Glass—smart glasses that were never adopted by the general public despite all the efforts Google's Mountain View, California-based research facility made to promote its ingenious discovery. This innovative tech development was more or less discontinued after two years, and for very specific reasons: its designers did not correctly identify how consumers would use it, and what would give them the "can't-live-without-it" feeling that would make it sell[26]. The company counted on its being perceived as a tech novelty, and settled for selling its visionary aspect to tech fanatics and journalists. But you can never hook customers on a product when you focus too much on a its technological specifications and too little on them.

---

25. Denise Lee Yohn, "Why Great Innovation Needs Great Marketing," *Hbr.org*, February 20, 2019.
26. *Ibid.*

Sony Reader versus the Kindle

This insensitivity to marketing issues also led to the failure of the Sony Reader, the first fully functioning e-book reader on the market. Unlike the Amazon Kindle, which had nothing particularly revolutionary about it, the Sony Reader never won over its clientele. Typical of what we like to call "product hypertrophy[27]," the Japanese group's e-reader was neither imagined nor marketed with the consumers' needs in mind.

First, Sony did not enlist the book-publishing industry as an ally to provide the needed content for the reader: "Sony hadn't tapped the customer and customer experience orientation inherent in marking to ensure the ecosystem around its product would be as well-developed and well-designed as the product itself[28]." As for the sales aspect, it was not adapted to potential buyers—people who read books. Distribution of the Sony Reader was organized via consumer electronics stores, as if it were a PlayStation console or a television set. Too busy inventing a reader that was technically flawless, Sony's teams ignored its customers… and unfortunately, they responded in kind.

4. JUUL, THE SYMBOL OF CALIFORNIAN *JUNK TECH*

Communication strategies that go against the grain

In contrast, the success of some companies is a direct result of the quality of their aspirational brand strategies. This was especially true for Juul Labs, an e-cigarette startup, which had a meteoric rise after its launch in May 2015. By late 2018, the company was valued at $38 billion—more than SpaceX or Airbnb—after its partial takeover by Altria, which

---

27. For more information, see Chapter IV.
28. Denise Lee Yohn, *op. cit.*

also owns Marlboro. In just three years, Juul had managed to capture more than 70 percent of the e-cigarette and vape market share in the United States, with products in the shape of USB sticks and flash drives and scented nicotine refill cartridges or "pods." Unlike its competitors, this Californian startup put in place a bold strategy to appeal to customers and young people that ran counter to the expected message. Instead of presenting its e-cigarettes as a tobacco substitute, it re-enchanted the figure of the smoker, who became an ad for "Life 2.0": free, connected young people, happy and proud to be "juuling[29]" with their friends. It was only after warnings from the American Food and Drugs Administration (FDA), worried about the increase in e-smoking in middle and high school, that Juul adjusted its marketing strategy and began talking about the fight to curb tobacco use. But the essential had already been accomplished. The company, with a hugely trendy product adopted by young consumers, had achieved its goal—developing a new kind of addiction.

Juul's tour de force seems all the more remarkable since cigarettes was perceived as very negative in the Western countries' collective psyche after a series of scandals rocked the tobacco industry. After that, smoking became "uncool"; the Marlboro Man, a triumphant America icon, has since become a distant memory. In order to win over people's hearts and minds and to establish new codes, Juul inroduced a narrative that empowers the consumer's ego: that of a young generation, festive, a bit rebellious, flaunting its inclusion in a community of fashionable people safely "juuling." Thanks to a cleverly orchestrated social media campaign, Juul's e-cigarettes

---

29. The neologism quickly imposed itself in the United States: "In American middle and high schools, you don't use an e-cigarette, you 'Juul.' And this is proudly displayed on Instagram and Snapchat. The opposite is true of cigarettes, whose consumption is steadily declining among American teenagers – fewer than 8% of high school students smoke." Jérôme Marin, "Aux États-Unis, on ne fume plus, on 'juule'," *Letemps.ch*, October 6, 2018.

fostered a viral phenomenon[30]. The company created product addiction that was founded less on physiological factors than on the ability to magnify millennials' dominant ideology and values: a cult of images, narcissism, a search for recognition within a "tribe[31]," an obsession with well-being and a "cool attitude[32]."

A product that is both aspirational and generational

In its own way, Juul recycled the methods used in the late 1920s by the American Tobacco Company to target women. At the time, women who smoked in public were singled out, and cigarette manufacturers were looking for an intelligent way to shatter the taboos associated with them. With the help of publicist Edward Bernays, a pioneer in public relations and the father of modern propaganda, they chose to associate cigarettes with the suffragettes fighting for equality for American women. To extol the merits of tobacco, they supported the liberation of women. In 1928, Bernays imagined a mise en scène somewhat reminiscent of the happenings organized today by feminist groups, who are often quite savvy about public relations. The day of the New York City Easter Parade, glamour girls were hired and dressed as suffragettes, who while marching would pull out cigarettes, light them and wave these "torches of freedom" in the air. The campaign became a milestone in American media; the event turned public opinion upside down.

---

30. Kathleen Chaykowski, "*The Disturbing Focus of Juul's Early Marketing Campaigns,*" *Forbes.com,* November 16, 2018.

31. Michel Maffesoli, *Le temps des tribus. Le déclin de l'individualisme dans les sociétés postmodernes,* Éditions de la Table Ronde, October 2000.

32. As the philosopher Benoît Heilbrunn notes, "The United States shifted from the rigor and moral rectitude of the Massachusetts 'Pilgrim Fathers' to the Californian 'cool attitude,' which finds its inspiration in Oriental philosophies." Jean-Marc Daniel, "La tyrannie de la 'cool attitude'," *Lexpansion.lexpress.fr,* March 27, 2019, Benoît Heilbrunn, *L'obsession du bien-être,* Robert Laffont, February 2019.

The taboo against women smoking in public disappeared, and the tobacco industry launched a dozen brands dedicated to its female clientele during the 1930s[33].

A symbol of Californian *junk tech*, Juul owes its success to its leaders' ingenious marketing intuition; they were able to decipher the uses and aspirations of millennials and teenagers. Although they are now busy defending themselves against the wrath of the FDA, the founders of this startup have exploited something no one in the electronic cigarette market had ever thought of. Quitting smoking is obviously beneficial from a health point of view, but it can also represent deprivation and loss, which is not a desirable goal nor a vector for personal fulfillment. In order to give its product an aspirational dimension, Juul had to offer something more, a product that was both a symbol of prestige and connected to a new generation.

The difficulties the company encountered in 2020, when it found itself unable to replicate in Europe what it had achieved in the United States, change nothing: a decline in business resulting from the arrival of such newcomers as Vuse on the scene, coupled with more stringent European regulations on nicotine levels, in no way invalidates the strength of Juul's value proposition and marketing skills. Its difficulties are more in line with the challenges associated with the advent of a world of constrained innovation in which there is less and less room for "laissez-faire." Whether in terms of data protection or health security, the government is increasingly attentive to the risks and negative externalities generated by certain products or services… especially when issues of trade wars are played out in the background[34].

Finally, it is certainly no accident that Juul emerged in Silicon Valley. In recent years, this part of the globe has

---

33. Jonah Sachs, *Winning the Story Wars. Why Those Who Tell—And Live—the Best Stories Will Rule the Future*, Harvard Business Review Press, July 2012.

34. For more information on this, see Chapter VII.

become the kingdom of *junk tech*, a movement that combines two trends: the talent to design highly addictive products and services; and the ability to make people believe that the comparative advantage of a Californian startup comes from technological superiority, when in reality it is rooted in the cultural factors of addiction and enchantment.

II.

THE DREAM PEDDLERS OF SILICON VALLEY

> "The myth of San Francisco [...] is back, the one that, from the twenty-first century, represented, in the national imagination, the ultimate horizon, the last stop, the providential west of a redemptive and redeeming America."
>
> ÉRIC SADIN,
> *La Silicolonisation* du *monde :*
> *L'irrésistible expansion du libéralisme*
> *(Pour en finir avec)*

In his essay on the United States in the mid-1980s, Jean Baudrillard, the French sociologist and philosopher, wrote, "In the image of Reagan, the whole of America has become Californian. Exactor and ex-governor of California that he is, he has worked up his euphoric, cinematic, extraverted, advertising vision of the artificial paradises of the West to all-American dimensions. He has introduced a system where the easy life exerts a kind of blackmail, reviving the original American pact of an achieved utopia[1]." At the time, Silicon Valley was not yet the promised land of geeks, startuppers and the heroes of the new economy. Few could have foreseen

---

1. Jean Baudrillard, *America*, Verso, 1988.

the incredible growth of this region of the globe[2], and it was only the beginning of a shift in the U.S. center of gravity from east to west. Baudrillard had anticipated the fact that after the moral crisis and disenchantment of the 1960s and 1970s, California would become the prime location for reviving the American dream. As with cinema out of Hollywood, one of the instruments of American soft power during the Cold War, the new technologies coming out of Silicon Valley would be transformed into a tool of cultural conquest. This is not surprising when you consider the links between these two industries: a few decades earlier, the first important client for Hewlett-Packard, founded in 1939, was none other than Walt Disney, who commissioned the computer company to create the special effects for *Fantasia*[3].

Baudrillard's portrait of the new elite seems in many ways to prefigure the emergence of Steve Jobs, Elon Musk, Larry Page, Peter Thiel, Marc Zuckerberg and all the children of the counterculture who participated in the digital revolution: "They are not the militants of happiness and success, but its sympathizers. The generation that has come from the sixties and seventies, but has rid itself of all nostalgia for, all bad conscience about, and even any subconscious memory of those wild years. The very last traces of marginality excised as if by plastic surgery: new faces, new fingernails, glossy brain-cells, the whole topped with a tousle of software. A generation neither fired by ambition nor fueled by the energy of repression, but

---

2. Nevertheless, in France we can find traces of some more technical works that already showed an interest in the dynamism and specificities of the California ecosystem: "The Silicon Valley is resisting the Japanese and making its mark in software, microcomputing and even office automation. California is at the crossroads of both worlds. It is the outpost of economic activity in the United States, and represents the non-decadent part of what we call the 'Western world.'" Martine Basset, *Silicon Valley. Les ressorts de l'avance californienne*, Éditions hommes et techniques, 1984.

3. Thierry Weil, "Des histoires de la Silicon Valley," *Entreprises et Histoire*, Eska, 2010.

completely refocused upon themselves, in love with business not so much for profit or prestige as for its being a sort of performance, a technical feat. They hover around the media, advertising, and computing[4]." However, what the French philosopher probably failed to anticipate was that Silicon Valley would itself come to embody this revival of the United States thanks to the invention of a new "artificial paradise"—*junk tech*, a soft power as habit-forming as hard drugs.

1. WHY DOES SILICON VALLEY DOMINATE THE WORLD?

Technological superiority: the making of a legend

For several years, companies based in Silicon Valley have managed to convince the entire world that their success comes from their technological superiority and creative genius. They developed a discourse that is particularly appealing to consumers and investors—tech "solutionism[5]," which promises that technology can re-enchant people's daily lives (through mobility, entertainment, e-commerce) and solve humanity's problems (fighting against death, global warming, conquering other planets). But this is partly an illusion. The media and the general public are victims of a collective hallucination whose adverse effects never seem to dissipate.

To keep people hooked on their products, the Silicon Valley entrepreneurs use a highly addictive substance—*junk tech*, which subtly combines the ability to tap into the zeitgeist, a grasp of people's aspirations, the talent to transform these two things into a highly coherent product or service and the power to shape myths that resonate with individual and collective desires. These business leaders have won the "story

---

4. Jean Baudrillard, *op. cit.*

5. Evgeny Morozov, *To Save Everything, Click Here: The Folly of Technological Solutionism*, PublicAffairs, July 2014.

wars[6]." In the digital civilization, dream peddlers and mirage merchants have taken over from engineers, developing a vision of the world that enables them to attract capital, talent and public attention, a world in which technology is only a means, never an end in itself.

In France, Europe and sometimes even the United States, many decision-makers are trying to reproduce the Silicon Valley formula but without the right ingredients. Convinced that good technology will be enough to conquer the market, too many companies and startups concentrate on product and end up omitting the essential: their customers' basic ambitions. By neglecting the art of storytelling and remaining captive to a technocentric approach, they adopt the wrong recipe: product hypertrophy, the cult of intellect, a rejection of simplicity, a dependency on rational approaches and a weak cooperative culture.

Anyone looking at the example of Silicon Valley will be struck by the mystery surrounding its success: how did this small agricultural valley, specialized in making small electronics and semiconductors during the twentieth century, located in a state with one of the country's highest tax rates, give birth to so many big names in the digital world? Why wasn't it Japan, a nation that dominated the high-tech world until the early 1990s, that benefitted from the digital economy's coming of age? From a Cartesian—and therefore French—viewpoint, all this seems quite unnatural.

But the interesting thing about Japan's trajectory is that it shows that technological superiority is not enough to build success, that it is no longer a determining factor in the aspirational age. The Japanese lost neither their know-how nor their incredible technical expertise, but they have not been able to adapt to the changing times: "Japan, which was well placed in new technologies until the 1980s and 1990s, fell behind [...]

____

6. Jonah Sachs, *op. cit.*

on the international digital scene because it was trapped by its perfectionism, so far removed from the GAFA's culture, a state of permanent beta. In addition, Japan, which is an industrial country, prefers to detail process rigorously or to have orders placed before developing it, which is potentially a hindrance to innovation[7]." The relative decline of the Empire of the Rising Sun can therefore be explained by cultural factors: in an era when it is necessary to move quickly and to anticipate consumer aspirations nonstop, operating methods based on technological perfectionism are ineffective in most sectors; they make no room for maximizing the value of what is produced. Nevertheless, these methods are still important in such traditional efficiency-based industries as the automotive industry, in which "Deutsche Qualität" (German quality) is a key factor in the success of a company's business, and the commitment to "zero defects" is a distinguishing factor. Even if marketing is not totally alien to the survival of this brand image[8]…

The origins of success: the pioneer spirit

Unlike the Japanese, Silicon Valley entrepreneurs have been able to rely on their DNA and their pioneer spirit to surf the new spirit of capitalism[9], to innovate without interruption, to overcome critiques of consumer society and to respond to people's quest for meaning in the twenty-first century. Without retracing the region's entire history, it should be noted that it is one of the youngest civilizations in the West. The rise of San Francisco did not occur until the years from 1847 to 1850, a pivotal moment when the gold rush was attracting a large

---

7. David Fayon, *Made in Silicon Valley. Du numérique en Amérique*, Pearson, June 2017.

8. Jean-Rémy Macchia, "Qualité des voitures allemandes : mythe, ou réalité?" *Francetvinfo.fr*, May 9, 2014.

9. Luc Boltanski, Eve Chiapello, *Le nouvel esprit du capitalisme*, Gallimard, 1999.

number of adventurers who left everything behind hoping to make a fortune. It was during this period that California was admitted to the Union and became the thirty-first American state[10].

This cultural foundation is still extremely present, at least in the form of an ideal of success, which can be defined as an extraordinary willingness to clear untamed lands, to brave virgin territory in order to unearth nuggets and find the best gold-bearing veins. A sense of initiative and a pioneer spirit are the hallmarks of a Siliconian ideology extremely different from the codes that prevail in France and Europe. To briefly summarize this, Silicon Valley entrepreneurs are not the spiritual heirs of farmers, devoted to their cultural heritage and committed to slowly harvesting the fruits of the earth. They are risk-takers whose energy comes from celebrating the self-made man who starts from nothing to attain great success. This is a characteristic feature of the Californian venture-capital ecosystem: it is not only conceived as "a funding scheme, as is generally believed in France, but also a motivation for getting rich, with money as a fair reward for merit, work and the risk incurred[11]." The available funds and their constantly increasing size result from positive performance; this logic that has predominated for several generations. Their liquidity did not just fall from the sky. Although a Frenchman was at the origin of the first venture capital structure created after the Second World War, France, and more generally Europe, have not necessarily been inspired by this philosophy[12].

---

10. Thierry Weil, *op. cit.*

11. Martine Basset, *op. cit.*

12. "The first modern venture capital firm, *American Research and Development* (ARD), was principally founded in 1946 by Karl Compton, President of MIT (Massachusetts Institute of Technology), and Georges Doriot, a French-born professor at Harvard [...] In 1958, the first venture capital company, Draper, Gaither & Anderson, The first modern venture capital firm, American Research and Development (ARD), was mainly created in 1946 by Karl Compton, President of MIT (Massachusetts Institute

There is nothing surprising about the fact that Silicon Valley dominates the venture-capital world and outperforms the American East Coast, once a cradle of technology entrepreneurship. In 1995, Silicon Valley accounted for 22.6 percent of American venture capital investments, compared to 9.9 percent for New England. It now represents more than 50 percent of these investments, while the Boston area has maintained its share around 10 percent. In addition to legal specificities, such as the absence of non-competition clauses in California, Silicon Valley "benefited from a more free-wheeling, less hierarchical and more risk-taking culture than New England." In addition, "as the market for private capital has grown and matured, new ventures can raise extremely large sums of capital without the necessity of a public listing[13]." No technological determinism is involved here.

Moreover, as the philosopher Eric Sadin explains, Silicon Valley entrepreneurs are in their own way the modern representatives of the Protestant ethic written about by Max Weber in his analysis of the development of capitalism. This state of mind "corresponds first to a specifically American tradition impregnated by a 'vernacular Protestantism' that glorified [...] individual initiative. Entrepreneurs [...] embodying the forces capable of contributing to the improvement of general living conditions and, more broadly, conforming to a teleological

---

of Technology), and Georges Doriot, a French Harvard professor. [...] In 1958 the first venture capital company, Draper, Gaither and Anderson, was founded, in the structure of a limited partnership (LP), which gradually became the dominant organizational form for raising funds to be invested in venture capital," and which proved to be more remunerative the more success it had. Ghizlane Kettani, Alain Villemeui, "Le capital-risque : un financement efficace de l'innovation sur le long terme," *Revue d'économie financière*, 2012/4 (n° 108).

13. Anil Gupta, Haiyan Wang, "The Reason Silicon Valley Beat Out Boston for VC Dominance", *Hbr.org*, November 15, 2016.

perspective, worked decisively for the 'humanity's salvation[14].'"
This quasi-divine ambition blends seamlessly with their pioneer
DNA and their ability to grasp people's dearest wishes. It can
be seen in the transhumanists (Larry Page, Peter Thiel) who
promise to deliver us from death; it can be seen with in Elon
Musk, who has taken the dreams of ending fossil fuels (Tesla,
SolarCity) and the colonizing Mars (SpaceX) and put them
at arm's length; and it is also palpable in the constitution
of a peaceful, united community, a community capable of
communicating in real time and without barriers (Facebook),
like humanity before the Tower of Babel.

The power of an entrepreneurial ecosystem, builder of a heroic narrative

The second reason for Silicon Valley's superiority lies in
the strength of the ecosystem that emerged around the universities of Stanford and Berkeley and around the semiconductor
industry, which benefited from investments made by the U.S.
military in the mid-twentieth century and during the Cold
War. A scientific military-industrial complex was formed in
the 1950s, just before the era of space exploration and the
Korean War, which created favorable conditions for innovation. Despite the drop in military spending in the following
decade, Silicon Valley benefited from the pump priming effect
of government funds[15]. The government's initial part in this
success story should be kept in mind. The discourse of liber-
tarians who exalt only the genius of certain individuals tends
to obliterate this reality, but without a doubt it played a role
in creating the myth of the Silicon Valley brand.

This was the point of view posited by Mariana Mazzucato
in *The Entrepreneurial State*. In her best-seller, published in

---

14. *La silicolonisation du monde. L'irrésistible ascension du libéralisme numérique*, L'échappée Éditions, October 2016.
15. Thierry Weil, *op. cit.*

2013, this Italian-American economist shows that funding from the U.S. government, starting with those of the Defense Advanced Research Projects Agency (DARPA) and the National Aeronautics and Space Administration (NASA), made it possible to finance all the procedures that subsequently gave rise to such innovations as the iPhone, the GPS, Internet infrastructure, the touch screen and more[16]. This is a constant that is also found in other countries. As soon as the vital interests of a nation come into play, the government invests in military technologies that sooner or later help the private sector, and high tech in particular. This does not mean that the government should oversee or administer innovation; its mission consists simply of generating positive externalities[17].

Israel as a startup nation, which has a general framework very similar to that of Silicon Valley, also followed this path. Government efforts in fundamental research and support for startups played a key role in establishing the ecosystem. Despite unfavorable geographic and geopolitical conditions, an impressive number of startups emerged in this tiny country. Israel was also able to rely on a risk culture and on innovation linked to its demographics. Most of its inhabitants are immigrants who settled there hoping to start over and build a better life; their journey brings them closer to the pioneering DNA of California's gold miners. Although for the moment Israel's greatest successes have been bought up by the American digital giants—such as Waze, which was bought out by Google—the country boasts more technological successes than Europe or Japan[18].

---

16. Mariana Mazzucato, *The Entrepreneurial State. Debunking Public vs. Private Sector Myths*, Anthem Press, June 2013.

17. In the United States, the venture capital ecosystem developed strongly from 1979 after the amendment of the Prudent Man Rule, which allowed pension funds to invest in risky assets. This regulatory evolution has been a powerful stimulus.

18. Dan Senor, Saul Singer, *Startup Nation. The Story of Israel's Economic Miracle*, Twelve, November 2009.

More generally, the planet's most innovative ecosystems are those that transform their cultural specificities into an economic asset and create a heroic narrative around it. In Silicon Valley, a sense of openness to the world, combined with the existence of powerful networks of like-minded entrepreneurs contributed to the region's development. Peter Thiel, who was a member of the famous "PayPal Mafia[19]," knows this better than anyone: it is now groupings of companies with cooperative and competitive relationships (coopetition) that are exerting a decisive influence on the business environment and the advent of breakthrough innovations. On the first pages of his book *From Zero to One*, he explains, "New technology tends to come from new ventures—startups. From the Founding Fathers in politics to the Royal Society in science to Fairchild Semiconductor's 'traitorous eight' in business, small groups of people bound together by a sense of mission have changed the world for the better[20]." While we may not entirely agree with this, a statement typical of the legend of Silicon Valley, we do find it accurate in that it testifies to the ability of a handful of entrepreneurs to change the rules of the game and impose business models that serve as a reference. It was in fact a group of eight people who left Shockley Semiconductor Laboratory in 1957 and became part of the Fairchild Semiconductor adventure, helping more than 120 Silicon Valley companies, including AMD and Intel, to flourish[21].

One of these "traitorous eight," Gordon Moore, is at the origin of the famous law of the same name. To explain it simply, it states that the number of transistors that can be

---

19. his is the nickname given to a group of former PayPal employees and founders who have since developed other technology companies such as Tesla, LinkedIn, Palantir, SpaceX, YouTube, Yelp and Yammer. Six of them became billionaires: Peter Thiel, Elon Musk, Reid Hoffman, Luke Nosek, Ken Howery and Keith Rabois.

20. Peter Thiel, *Zero to One: Notes on Startups, or How to Build the Future*, Crown Business, September 2014.

21. Thierry Weil, *op. cit.*

fit on a computer chip will double every eighteen months, resulting in periodic increases in computing power. Even if it is more a self-fulfilling prophecy than a physical rule, Moore's Law is still one of the founding narratives of Silicon Valley. What used to be a selling point for Intel became a popular and newsworthy belief: the California engineers would have a major technological lead over their competitors. The addictive mechanisms of *junk tech* were already at work with this pseudo-scientific statement. By fueling the idea that the performance of their hardware would be consistently regenerated, the first Silicon Valley gurus created an irresistible appetite for their products. Steve Jobs did just this during his keynote speeches, in which he managed to convince his audience that the latest iPhone or iPad model was utterly revolutionary.

In short, Silicon Valley's success rests on three cornerstones: a fertile cultural ground for innovation; sources of funding that are constantly increasing thanks to the performance and success of capital risk; a sense of storytelling that is ingrained in the mindset of the region's entrepreneurs, who have been able to reenchant the American dream and build an intelligent nation branding building strategy. This is the meaning of "world Silicolonilization" as evoked by French philosopher Éric Sadin. Silicon Valley is more than a place: it is an ideal, a myth, an ideology that revives the fantasy of the California gold rush and exerts an immensely powerful appeal around the globe[22]. Fabien Benoît, a French journalist, makes a similar observation in his recent book *The Valley*, which examines the political project of the companies of this "tech mecca[23]."

---

22. Éric Sadin, *op. cit.*

23. Fabien Benoît, *The Valley. Une histoire politique de la Silicon Valley*, Les Arènes, May 2019.

2. THE LOST WORLD:
WHAT IS BECOMING OF EUROPE AND ASIA?

An irrevocable decline?

In the decades to come, American or Chinese tourists may see Europe and Japan as distant civilizations that disappeared from the international scene. In-between curiosity and astonishment, they will wonder how those countries managed to go from the heights of innovation and world leadership to the charming but unenviable status of museums in such a short time; their travels will seem as exotic as a voyage to Jurassic Park or Easter Island…

We are being intentionally provocative here in order to emphasize a contemporary anomaly. In less than thirty years, Europe and Japan have been outclassed by America's West Coast. On the "Old Continent," the situation is grave: the technological business models that made so many companies famous in the early 1990s have since collapsed. The time when European companies dominated the telecommunications world, when they were at the forefront of innovation, may not be so distant, but now seems to belong to another age. In France, despite the number of startups launched each year, very few of these companies succeed in becoming "unicorns." Having once been "the champions of technologies that are truly remarkable, but never really make inroads (calculation schemes, micro-computers), cannot be exported (Minitel, Concorde) or are very difficult to export (TGV, smart cards) [24]," the French are losing their ability to imagine disruptive innovations. We are still anchored in a system that worships inventors and inventions[25]. Some commentators, such as French entrepreneur, essayist and thinker Laurent Alexandre,

---

24. Jean-Baptiste Rudelle, *On m'avait dit que c'était impossible. Le manifeste du fondateur de Criteo*, Stock, 2015.
25. For more information on this, see Chapter v.

predict that Europe will eventually become a digital colony of the United States and China. The picture may therefore seem hopeless. Europeans have missed the step separating consumer society from the aspirational age; they continue to favor a culture of efficiency in a world being taken over by cultural affinity[26].

But if you look at the history of science and innovation from a long-term perspective, you can see that a nation's decline or triumph is not inevitable, nor, as we have already said, is there any technological determinism. More often than not, political explanations and choices based on social attitudes come into play. Until the mid-fifteenth siècle, for example, China had a definite lead over Europe. It had developed revolutionary inventions for humanity: printing, papermaking, kites, boat rudders, cast iron, sluice gates, gunpowder… From this point of view, the so-called Middle Kingdom should have set out to conquer the world at the time of the great discoveries. In fact, this was ambitioned by Admiral Zheng He, who led the Chinese fleets that explored the Red Sea, the eastern coasts of Africa and the Indian Ocean, but never happened.

When China fell asleep … then woke up

In the fifteenth siècle, the imperial court was divided between two rival factions: the Confucianists, who sought to preserve the ancient order, and the eunuchs such as Zheng He, who led huge fleet in the world on several expeditions. When Zheng He died, the Confucianists convinced the Emporer that the voyages were too costly, banned the construction of ships and prohibited all maritime endeavors. These seemingly insignificant decisions led the country into a period of isola-tionism that led to its losing its capacity for innovation and its supremacy, initiating a decline that would last several

---

26. For more information on this, see Chapter III.

centuries. China cut itself off from this turning point in the age of globalization, while Christopher Columbus' Europe was just taking off[27].

Inversely, we should keep in mind that China's awakening in the twentieth century began after Mao's death in 1976, when Deng Xiaoping made it possible for China to break out of its self-imposed isolation and open up to foreign investment and technology. By shifting to a cycle of openness, the Chinese leader put his country back on the path towards progress and innovation. Since the late 1970s, China has passed through all the stages of development, and established itself as an essential player in the field of new technologies—so much so that it is now Silicon Valley's only serious rival, as can be seen in the dramatic arrival in the digital galaxy of BATX (Baidu, Alibaba, Tencent, Xiami).

According to the Taiwanese investor Kai-Fu Lee, who was head of Google China among other things, China is rising so rapidly in the field of digital and artificial intelligence that it will eventually match or even overtake the United States[28]. According to him, explains Mariane Kone, "AI is at a stage in its development where fundamental research—an area where Americans outperform the Chinese—is less important than 'brute force advancement.' In other words, China is winning the war not because their AI is better, but because they have the ability to implement it in a wide range of applications. China has an army of 'pretty good' computer scientists and a billion people connected to test the applications of their AI[29]."

Aggressive and skillful, Chinese entrepreneurs have the opportunity to operate in a market that remains relatively

---

27. Jared Diamond, *Guns, Germs, and Steel: The Fates of Human Societies*, W. W. Norton & Company, April, 1999.

28. Kai-Fu Lee, *AI Superpowers. China, Silicon Valley, and the New World Order*, Houghton Mifflin Harcourt, September 2018.

29. Mariane Kone, "Conseil de lecture : '*AI Superpowers*' de Lee Kai-Fu," *Portail-ie.fr*, December 6, 2018.

deregulated despite the influence of the government: they are not subject to any constraints related to ethics, privacy or the General Data Protection Regulations (GDPR). They can push the experimental devices and the sacrosanct logic of the test and learn approach much further and on a larger scale than their Californian and European counterparts. They have learned from Silicon Valley's successes and are radicalizing its precepts. Perhaps they are even the only ones to have understood that pure technological superiority was only a decoy and that other factors enter into the complex equation that links innovation and public adoption.

The question is whether the Chinese will be able to win the race of uses on a global scale. Unlike the Japanese, they can count on a large diaspora to "colonize" other countries by spreading their cultural and technological practices. But there is nothing to say that this race is a foregone conclusion. Unlike the American dream exported from Silicon Valley—which is sometimes tarnished by resounding scandals (Cambridge Analytica, the Uber data breach…)—Chinese technology is more like a nightmare for a whole section of Western public opinion sensitive to the risks of a digital dictatorship and "no limit[30]" imperialism; what is "made in China" is not necessarily in line with the rising values of the emerging technological civilization. It is not certain that such an image promotes the penetration of innovations made in China and meets the aspirations of 2.0 individuals. Unless their narcissism leads them to forget these threats and dissipates the legitimate fears of China's stranglehold on the digital ecosystem…

---

30. *Usbek & Rica*, "Chine : l'Empire no limit," n° 22, May 2018.

III.

From the consumer society to the aspirational age: the triumph of Narcissus?

> "Having no hope of improving their lives in any of the ways that matter, people have convinced themselves that what matters is psychic self-improvement: getting in touch with their feelings, eating health food, taking lessons in ballet or belly-dancing, immersing themselves in the wisdom of the East, jogging, learning how to 'relate,' overcoming the 'fear of pleasure.'"
>
> Christopher Lasch,
> *The Culture of Narcissism.*
> *American Life in an Age*
> *of Diminishing Expectations*

In December 2018, Netflix went a step further in personalizing content by offering subscribers a fully interactive episode of the series "Black Mirror." Entitled *Bandersnatch*, the film offers viewers multiple choices based on the principles of the interactive *Choose Your Own Adventure* books, a popular teen series from the 1980s. *Bandersnatch* invites the viewer to assume the role of Stefan Butler, a young computer scientist obsessed with designing a video game by adapting a fantasy gamebook in which the reader guides the course of the game through a series of individual decisions. The story and the outcome of the episode are shaped by the choices made by the viewer for Stefan. *Bandersnatch* goes beyond an entertaining mise en abyme; it is above all based on an effective strategy for hooking[1] and ensnaring viewers: creating the feeling they are living a unique experience, giving them the impression they themselves are demiurges controlling the series, and providing incentive for them to watch the episode several times in order to discover alternative endings.

This example demonstrates the four mechanisms that make up the hook model, which draws on methodology from behavioral science, used by companies and social media to manufacture desire and create habit-forming products: a "trigger" that invites or cues the user to take action; the "action" or behavior; and the "variable reward" that ensues, pushing the user into the "investment" phase. This pattern of digital addiction following this logic generates compulsive behavior in the consumer[2].

1. THE REVOLUTION: IS IT TECHNOLOGICAL OR ANTHROPOLOGICAL?

First steps in empowerment marketing

All these ingredients create a particularly addictive cocktail that appeals to the viewer's ego while cultivating an affinity with Netflix. The video streaming platform understood that

---

1. The techniques of "phishing" or cognitive "hooking" are today a well-documented subject, notably by Israeli-American entrepreneur Nir Eyal, who has shown how social networks and digital champions are using neuroscience knowledge to keep users addicted to reward-based devices. Nir Eyal, *Hooked. How to Build Habit-Forming Products*, Portfolio Penguin, November 2014.

2. Ted Greenwald, *"Compulsive Behavior Sells,"* *MIT Technology Review*, March 23, 2015.

we're all Narcissus seeking recognition and content that relates to our most secret thoughts. By projecting us into 1984 and in Stefan's shoes, which then mirrors our dependence on technological devices and our anxiety about being under constant surveillance, Netflix skillfully addresses today's individual and collective psychology. Whatever you may think of *Bandersnatch*'s artistic qualities, the episode is an excellent reflection of the contradictions of the citizen-consumer hybrid[3] in the aspirational age. Stefan Butler is us!

In this episode, Netflix liberally adopted the codes of Apple's famous television commercial for the 1984 Super Bowl, designed for the launch of the first Macintosh. In the video, inspired by an Orwellian universe, an army of workers—all clonelike and clad in gray—are hypnotized by a large screen broadcasting Big Brother giving a speech. An athletic, rebellious-looking young woman emerges; pursued by soldiers, she sprints toward the auditorium brandishing a sledgehammer, which she flings at the screen, destroying it and awakening the masses from their stupor, dispelling their illusions and leading the way from the darkness of conformism to the triumph of individual creativity. The logo, an apple with a bite taken out of it in the colors of the rainbow, then appears. You don't have to be a genius to decipher the meaning of this ad.

Although "Think different" was not yet Apple's slogan, the message was already there. With this commercial, Steve Jobs' firm promised consumers to awaken the hero slumbering inside them, to give them the keys to an extraordinary world,[4] marking the emergence of empowerment marketing, which stimulates people's desire for autonomy and singularity. Like other companies, Apple created a mythology around its products by telling its customers a story that promotes their self-esteem; it not only rewards them for having the attention

---

3. For more information on this, see *below*.
4. Jonah Sachs, *op. cit.*

span of "goldfish"[5]; to extend the metaphor, it also incites them to break out of the fish tank, to break the mold, in order to access a world consistent with their deepest desires, their psyches, their authentic "self"—which is perhaps a more skillful and insidious way to lock them into another mold.

In some ways, that first Apple commercial was visionary. Television, the cult object of the consumer society, would gradually be dethroned by the computer screen, tablet and smartphone, symbol of the aspirational age. But it would be wrong to reduce this change to a technological breakthrough. That which has been going on for more than thirty years, becoming more pronounced under the effect of digital innovations, is a cultural, even anthropological upheaval. Without necessarily realizing it, we have shifted from a world of ants to a world of grasshoppers.

From the world of ants to that of grasshoppers

The consumer society of the France's Trente Glorieuses was a kingdom of ants, of Cartesian and rational beings whose sense of individualism was tempered by belonging to traditional communities that served as markers of identity and vectors of identification: family, religion, city, business, childhood friends, leisure clubs, and so on. Ants came from a long evolutionary process that began in the Enlightenment with the advent of more autonomy for people and the gradual extinction of societies from the Ancien Régime, the social system in which people were assigned places at birth according to natural law. The nineteenth and early twentieth centuries extended this process and allowed citizens to progressively assert their free will, but this individualist revolution took place within a framework until the 1960s. Ways of life were still structured

---

5. Bruno Patino, *La civilisation du poisson rouge. Petit traité sur le marché de l'attention*, Grasset, April 2019.

by traditional communities, forcing everyone to conform to a kind of social discipline[6].

Starting in the 1960s, several phenomena coalesced to give birth to a new generation that ultimately led to the Narcissus of the year 2020. Critiques of consumer society, the counter-culture offensive, the loosening of morals, the decline of historical meaning[7], an emphasis on personal development and the evolution of educational methods—all led to challenging the prevailing norms. Whether you celebrate these changes or detest them, they have had a huge impact on people's behavior and the way in which they fulfill their ambitions. There is no turning back.

In a 1979 book whose content now seems prophetic, Christopher Lasch, an American historian, analyzed the shift towards widespread pathological narcissism and a world in which individuals deeply believe they are the unequivocal center of the universe and the measure of all things: "The good opinion of friends and neighbors, which formerly informed a man that he had lived a useful life, rested on appreciation of his accomplishments. Today men seek the kind of approval that applauds not their actions but their personal attributes. They wish to be not so much esteemed as admired. They crave not fame but the glamour and excitement of celebrity. They want to be envied rather than respected. Pride and acquisitiveness, the sins of an ascendant capitalism, have given way to vanity[8]." Had he seen today's reality-show participants or the Instagram-obsessed, Christopher Lasch probably wouldn't have changed a word. Perhaps he had already anticipated these phenomena when he wrote that "modern life is so thoroughly

---

6. Jean-Claude Kaufmann, *L'invention de soi. Une théorie de l'identité*, Fayard/Pluriel, 2010.

7. Mathias Roux, *La dictature de l'ego. En finir avec le narcissisme de masse*, Larousse, November 2018.

8. Christopher Lasch, *The Culture of Narcissism. American Life in an Age of Diminishing Expectations*, W.W. Norton & Co, January 1979.

mediated by electronic images that we cannot help responding to others as if their actions—and our own—were being recorded and simultaneously transmitted to an unseen audience or stored up for close scrutiny at some later time[9]." In the age of digital everything and social networks, this now seems obvious, but forty years ago, it was just an emerging trend. The Internet and smartphone revolution, although is not at the origin of this transformation in the way people think, has both facilitated and accelerated it, and constitutes a response to consumers' new expectations.

The millennials and members of the "iGen[10]" who spend their lives glued to Snapchat did not magically appear in the digital world. They are the heirs of the generation that grew up in the 1970s, when the educational methods devised by baby-boomers revolved around their children's self-esteem. Influenced by self-improvement theories, convinced that their approach would maximize their offspring's chances for success, many parents instilled principles that made their children the center of attention. They were made to believe they were "special or a princess or a rock star," and they became adults who were perpetually dissatisfied, persuaded that their deepest aspirations were thwarted by the world around them[11].

In their quest for psychic fulfillment and self-actualization, this generation developed narcissistic personality traits that

---

9. *Ibid.*

10. "iGen is a neologism by psychologist Jean M. Twenge used to refer to people born from 1995 onward, who 'grew up with cell phones, had an Instagram account before entering high school and don't remember the time before Internet.'" Annabelle Laurent, "La 'génération iPhone' est-elle si différente des précédentes?" *Usbeketrica.com*, October 26, 2018, Jean M. Twenge, *iGen. Why Today's Super-Connected Kids Are Growing Up Less Rebellious, More Tolerant, Less Happy – and Completely Unprepared for Adulthood – and What That Means for the Rest of Us*, Atria Books, September 2018.

11. Joel Stein, "Millennials: The Me Me Me Generation. Why millennials will save us all," *Time.com*, May 20, 2013.

had a direct influence on consumer patterns, brand strategies, criteria for differentiating products and services and more. As we evoked previously, Apple and a few other pioneers in Silicon Valley were precursors when it came to understanding that the consumer society had shifted to the aspirational age. These companies were among the first to evolve and to adapt their value proposition to new, more individualistic norms[12]. Empowerment marketing is only one facet of *junk tech*: a way to give a healthy dose self-esteem to people who have been breastfed on admiration and think they lack recognition.

As several research studies have confirmed, millennials and representatives of the iGen have extended this movement. To use a provocative and fashionable term, they are "radicalized" narcissists. Technology has reinforced this psychological disposition. According to data from the National Institutes of Health in the U.S., narcissistic personality disorder is about three times higher in young people in their twenties than in people over sixty-five. In addition, 40 percent of millennials feel that their skills and talent are not sufficiently appreciated by the companies where they work[13]. At the same time, phenomena of loneliness and withdrawal are on the rise: between 2000 and 2015, while the number of teenagers going out with friends daily has dropped by 40 percent. According to Jean M. Twenge, professor of psychology and author of extensive research on the habits of young people, "This might be the most definitive evidence that iGen'ers spend less time interacting with their peers face-to-face than any previous generation—it's not just parties or craziness but merely getting together with friends, spending time hanging out. That's something nearly everyone

---

12. "Capitalism has skillfully integrated the counterculture into its ideology at the same time as some of their leaders let themselves be recuperated by the different powers, the itinerary of Apple's founder, Steve Jobs, representing the perfect example of the conjunction of these trends." Mathias Roux, *op. cit.*

13. Joel Stein, *op. cit.*

does: nerds and jocks, introverted teens and extroverted ones, poor kids and rich kids, C students and A students, stoners and clean-cut kids. It doesn't have to involve spending money or going someplace cool—it's just being with your friends. And teens are doing it much less[14]." The skating rink, the basketball court, the city's swimming pool, the local fishing spot have been replaced by virtual spaces accessible through applications and the web where teenagers can at all moments juggle friends, entertainment and communities without impeding their immediate desires. These are signs that don't lie.

In fact, we have now entered the world of grasshoppers. People want total autonomy and take from their various communities only what interests them, depending on fashions and trends: an individual can be "a defender of the Breton culture but also a computer scientist very involved in his work, a trade unionist faithful to his commitments and an impassioned scuba diver in the Indian Ocean. He is never all thses at once, he reactivates these different facets depending on moments and situations, in connection with universes, value systems, and specific people[15]." Digital technology broadens this field of possibilities, leading to an explosion in the number of communities and a much greater volatility of uses and modes of consumption. In the "society of ways of life" described by the sociologist Jean Viard, "each of us has multiple networks of relationships, within and outside the family, which have little by little overwhelmed the rare and rigid links of yesterday's world[16]." Freed from their traditional shackles, these grasshoppers 2.0 have plenty of time to leap around.

---

14. Jean M. Twenge, *iGen. Why Today's Super-Connected Kids Are Growing Up Less Rebellious, More Tolerant, Less Happy – and Completely Unprepared for Adulthood – and What That Means for the Rest of Us, op. cit.*

15. Jean-Claude Kaufmann, *op. cit.*

16. Jean Viard, *Nouveau portrait de la France. La société des modes de vie,* L'Aube, January 2012.

They also "swarm," to borrow the term used by philosopher Byung Chul-Han[17]: they can scatter as quickly as they congregated; they allow themselves to be affected by emotion and their endlessly fluctuating desires; they feed new conformities that benefit the organizations and brands that are most skillful. Unlike those of the Cartesian ants, the grasshoppers' expectations are much more difficult to anticipate and satisfy, creating increasing difficulties for companies.

Companies can no longer rely solely on the efficiency and power that were previously markings of the consumer society. Take the difficulties of superstores, for instance, once the symbol of a period when customers were "always looking for the best price," and when "products resembled each other from one brand to the next": "This model had its raisons d'être, its positive effects and its benefits for the economy and for employment[18]," but this is no longer necessarily in keeping with people's values in the twenty-first century. For professionals in the retail and food industry, one of the challenges is to introduce a sense of affinity[19], a connection with clients: to help them eat better, locally grown and organic food; to facilitate their purchases and save them time by releasing them from the drudgery of shopping; to make them feel that their personal well-being is the company's main concern, and so on. In short, they must think about fulfilling their aspirations rather than their shopping carts. When Narcissus shops in a supermarket or via a smartphone, he is not doing it just to have something to eat; he wants to conform to a concept of an ideal life. He is no longer dealing with primary needs, but is instead on the highest level of Maslow's hierarchy.

---

17. Byung Chul-Han, *In the Swarm: Digital Prospects, (Untimely Meditations)*, MIT Press, April 2017.
18. Jean-Claude Mochet, *Affinité*, Débats Publics, February 2019.
19. *Ibid.*

2. Mass narcissism versus mass individualism?

Reinforcing the dynamics of narcissism

The digital revolution has sustained this narcissistic dynamic in at least two ways. First, the products' or services' ergonomics and simplicity, which are becoming the essential vectors of their adoption by customers. Co-founder of the TheFamily, an accelerator created in Paris, Nicolas Colin, rightly points out that "we have entered a new cycle of innovation dominated by design, of working on user experience, simplification of complexity, resonance with the vibration of the multitude, all properties that are embodied not in technologies—which merely liberate innovation—but in applications based on experience and interaction[20]." Such characteristics flatter the consumer's ego. The simpler a product is to use, the smarter the user feels. With rare exceptions, increasing the number of a product's features and options is counterproductive. In consumer society, this could justify a higher price. In the aspirational age, this discourages the good intentions of a Narcissus who no longer has time to waste on seemingly over-sophisticated innovations. Technology no longer has a primary role but has become a secondary function.

Second, there is the question of speed. Companies such as Amazon and Uber have made us accustomed to immediate availability. The idea of "everything right now" has become the leitmotif of our lives. It seems banal to repeat it, but we can no longer bear waiting for anything at all. The frenzied satisfying of our needs seems to happen naturally, as if the ecosystem around us were yielding to them rather than the other way around.

Companies have to integrate this change. Consumers are increasingly turning to products and services that quench their narcissistic thirst. This trend can be felt at all levels,

---

20. Nicolas Colin, Henri Verdier, *L'âge de la multitude. Entreprendre et gouverner après la révolution numérique*, Armand Colin, May 2015.

even when individual behavior might seem to be guided by some kind of superior ethic. The urban population's enthusiasm for ecology and responsible consumption is a perfect illustration of this. The fact that citizens are taking up issues such as global warming, the negative effects of pollution or the harmful effects of junk food is excellent news for current and future generations. But it would no doubt be naïve to equate or reduce this change in mentality to a sudden shift in interest in the common good. For a certain number of those preoccupied by the ecology of everyday life and others obsessed by the small gestures intended to save the planet, there is first of all the will to please oneself, from a position of doing good deeds. They pay for a good conscience, for a kind of salvation, the way people used to buy things for self-gratification.

More generally, we thrive in a universe where the search for new transcendence and a supposedly harmonious lifestyle is invading social practices—especially among metropolitan and connected populations. Here again, there is no shortage of examples pas: yoga, which has become more a marketing invention than an ancestral Hindu practice and tends to resemble a "top hits menu for spirituality[21]"; running (more aspirational than jogging in the 1980s), a modern variant of *anima sana in corpore sano*[22] (a sound mind in a sound body), which represent the art of living for such brands as Nike, Adidas or Asics, which promise to transport us to an endorphin-filled paradise; mindfulness, a lucrative business popularized by a molecular biologist who democratized access to nirvana with a strange combination of Buddhism, psychotherapy and personal development[23]; veganism and anti-speciesism, which attract animal lovers, gentle utopians and more radical activists working for

----

21. Marie Kock, *Yoga, une histoire-monde*, La Découverte, March 2019.

22. Maximus of the Roman poet Juvenal (in its canonical form is "mens sana in corpore sano"), which inspired the acronym of the sports brand Asics.

23. The founder of this discipline is the American medical professor Jon Kabat-Zinn, born in 1944.

the reconciliation of species and the liberation of animals. In sum, other "gods" have now integrated the pantheon of our secularized existence. Other superstitions are replacing those of yesterday's world. Other synthetic drugs, seemingly milder, serve as palliatives to chronic dissatisfaction. They give us the feeling that we are touching the substantial marrow of our aspirations… which benefits all the companies that have been able to wrap their marketing in a spiritualist package.

By the late 1960s, when the foundations of consumer society were being undermined by the counterculture, this movement was in its infancy. The critique of our "bourgeois" and consumerist lifestyles never gave birth to a political and economic revolution. Rather, it offered a breath of fresh air to the of dreams peddlers and the merchants of mirages[24]. Woodstock was one of the first symptoms of this shift. According to David Dalton, an American journalist who attended the legendary music festival, "Woodstock was a hippie Disneyland, a triumph of public relations and old-fashioned merchandising perpetrated on unwitting, stoned trolls in denim jeans and faded T-shirts, […] a parade of juvenile breasts and buttocks, supposedly to show how uninhibited we were. But what are images really all about? Nothing more than a huge Coca-Cola commercial on Life[25]" replayed by thrill-seeking apprentice Narcissus. The criticism may be harsh, but there is some truth in it.

---

24. In the late 1960s in particular, "the counterculture movement began to believe that technology can be synonymous with emancipation, or even elevation of the spirit, in the same way as LSD. The meetings between researchers from university laboratories - those at Stanford in particular - and actors of the counterculture multiplied." Fabien Benoit, "Le Grateful Dead a-t-il inventé la Silicon Valley?" *Usbeketrica.com*, July 6, 2019.

25. Laurent Rigoulet, "À Woodstock, il pleut des cordes," *Télérama*, n° 3624, July 29, 2019.

A post-liberal society?

This is not about passing moral judgment on this transformation of our mores. What is certain, though, is that the rise of narcissism is not the same as an individualist revolution. On the contrary, it is likely that this trend will be accompanied by a decline in the values that have long structured liberal societies: property, security and freedom, which in theory are inalienable individual rights. In keeping with what Christopher Lasch predicted, we need "to distinguish the figure of the individualist of yesteryear (inherited from the America's pioneer culture), for whom the world is to be subjected to his will […] from the contemporary Narcissus, for whom the world is above all a mirror in which to contemplate his image. […] Now is the time of mass narcissism[26]." We can go even further by saying that many consumers are ready to jeopardize or sacrifice their individual rights (property, security, freedom) to enjoy the benefits of *junk tech* (simplicity, fluidity, immediacy, ego enhancement). In our post-materialist societies, we have become accustomed to seeing our physiological needs and our safety and security needs met, as if this were a given, an imprescriptible right. By focusing almost exclusively on self-esteem and self-fulfillment—which are at the top of Maslow's hierarchy of needs—we may well give up some of our essentials.

The sense of ownership has obviously not disappeared, but it has become less and less central since the emergence of apps based on sharing, collaboration, dematerialization or one-time consumption. On paper, there is no need to buy cars (BlaBlaCar, Drivy), records and CDs (Deezer, Spotify) or fixed office space (WeWork) to meet our mobility, entertainment or workspace needs. As for digital platforms (Uber, Airbnb) that have reached stock market valuations comparable or higher than those of the industrial giants of the past, they demonstrate

---

26. Mathias Roux, *op. cit.*

that it is possible—at least for the moment—to prosper without owning any physical assets.

In terms of security and freedom, the equation seems more complex. As citizens living in a democracy, we are all very attached to those values and claim to cherish them as our most precious assets. But as consumers and users of digital services, we actually give them negligible importance. Despite the recurring debates on the protection of our private data and the scandals that have hit companies such as Facebook, how many of us would seriously consider giving up social media? Despite Google's hold on the digital ecosystem and its knowledge of everyone's privacy, how many Europeans prefer Qwant? Despite the negative effects generated by the eruptive flow of vehicles and goods in cities (population congestion, pollution, "the share-the-scraps economy[27]" and the development of microwork, violations of social rights, etc.), how many city dwellers addicted to VTC or à la carte delivery would be ready to stop using Uber or Amazon? Despite the lack of proof as to the solidity of online banks, how many customers worry about the security of their funds when they open an account with N26 or Revolut? Such are the contradictions—such is the schizophrenia—of the citizen-consumer.

Similarly, we all feel that we are living something unique and that our experiences are personalized—while in reality we are increasingly surrounded by technology and analyzed as standard profiles, rather than as special, original, separate individuals. The smartphone, which has become an extension of ourselves, has contributed to this evolution: "we highlighted the possibility it offers to connect to the Internet at any time in any place, [… and] the narcissism it promotes, especially through the use, often compulsive, of selfies, we were alarmed by the addictive effects caused by all its charms […]. What was long overlooked was that, as if by a miracle, people were

---

27. Expression used by Bill Clinton's former Secretary of Labor Robert Reich. "The Share-the-Scraps Economy," *robertreich.org*, February 2, 2015.

no longer left to their own devices, to their own daily experience, but that they were surreptitiously taken over by these same pieces of equipment[28]" and guided in their choices by the power of data. The future success of AI, of IVAs and IPAs, depends on this parameter: their relevance and effectiveness depend on behavioral models obtained from a huge amount of data and recurrent use. Digital devices all appear to be hyper-customized, but they are much less so than we can even imagine. We adopt them without question because they seem to fit perfectly with our aspirations.

The other side of the mirror: the fear of collapse

If for consumers, mass narcissism and *junk tech* can induce euphoria, they also produce side effects in the collective consciousness. In a world that is gradually abandoning the basics, it is hardly surprising that the fear of collapse is spreading in people's minds. The popularity of books dealing with collapsology, survivalism's return to grace and libertarian projects for exile (artificial islands, secure bunkers in New Zealand…) are just some manifestations of this anxiety that is affecting our psyches, and what's more, at a time when global warming and the threat of a pandemic are fueling more concrete fears.

Seen from this viewpoint, the fear that took hold in people's minds during the Covid-19 epidemic is not surprising. By plunging us into a scenario straight out of a science-fiction film, this crisis has proven to be "viral" at all levels. The media hysteria and the fear contagion reflect a technological society governed by *junk tech*. The flood of opinions on issues people still knew nothing about—starting with the effects of hydroxychloroquine—and the adoption of new habits in record time (lockdown, wearing masks, etc.) followed a curve as rapid and exponential as the virus itself, without rational

---

28. Éric Sadin, *L'intelligence artificielle ou l'enjeu du siècle. Anatomie d'un antihumanisme radical*, L'Échappée, October 2018.

facts totally justifying this frenzy, this terror. Echoing fears that are both primal and rooted in the contemporary imagination, this crisis has awakened both our survival instinct and the death drive.

Even zombie movies have integrated this anxiety and inflected their message. In 1978, when director George A. Romero filmed four people thrust into a post-apocalyptic universe, he took up the codes and questions of consumerist society: the heroes were locked in a supermarket and chased by the undead, who in a rather transparent metaphor symbolized alienated consumers. Today, the protagonists of *The Walking Dead* and of other zombie programs are returning to the laws of the jungle; they doubt their own humanity and are hardly distinguishable from the monsters around them. The narrative of *The Walking Dead* is that of a civilized world on a very bad trip: there are no more property rights, except for the fittest; no more security, except for the best armed communities; no more real freedom outside of the tribes that are made and broken, according to the whims of fate. All landmarks having collapsed, the characters are forced to return to the fundamentals to survive.

The dystopian imagination of *The Walking Dead* series is a direct translation of the more or less irrational fears that arise in the aspirational age—in a way, the other side of the mirror, the dark glow of Narcissus' triumph. Every era is haunted by nightmares that speak volumes about its ideological substratum and its driving forces. In the consumer society, we were afraid of becoming "zombies" obsessed with our comfort of life and the enjoyment of material goods. In the aspirational age, we fear that our civilization is collapsing because we sense that to some extent it is built on fantasies, mirages and technological illusions.

This is in part the theory posited by Robert Gordon, an American economist, who argues that over the past forty years, innovation has brought very few gains and growth has slowed down and that the fruits of innovation were largely harvested before the mid-1970s[29]. In the age of *junk tech*, a question of this nature deserves to be heard and to be extended beyond the economic sphere. How much productivity growth really exists? What real improvement is occurring in health care, how much decline in major illnesses? What good is being accomplished for the environment and people's well-being? On all these subjects, it is not certain that progress is commensurate with the technological explosion touted by specialists and tech gurus. At the same time, increasing stress levels, falling IQs, the weakening of democracy and the proliferation of technological dependency reveal the side effects of *junk tech*: a model that succeeds on the financial and marketing level, but fails to bring positive transformations to the world.

Yet at this stage, it is not the champions of *junk tech* who have been caught in the trap of narcissism. Rather, it is the victims of industrial disasters (GE, Nokia, Kodak, etc.) who have fallen into this: lost in the flattering reflection of their past successes, they ended up drowning in their business model and denied themselves a vision for the future. Conversely, in recent years, some large companies and startups have taken advantage of the distortion in the supply chain and the transformation in their industry. To find the right strategy for positioning themselves, they avoided four errors: product hypertrophy, the cult of intellect, dependence on rational approaches and the startup's magical thinking.

---

29. Robert J. Gordon, *The Rise and Fall of American Growth. The U.S. Standard of Living since the Civil War*, Princeton University Press, February 2016.

IV.

Ending Product Hypertrophy: Building a Coherent Offer

> "Marketing is so basic that it is not just enough to have a strong sales department and to entrust marketing to it. Marketing is not only much broader than selling; it is not a specialized activity at all. It encompasses the entire business. It is the whole business seen from the point of view of its final result, that is from the customer's point of view."
>
> Peter Drucker

Who remembers the Californian startup Juicero? Founded in 2013, the company managed to raise $120 million from such prestigious venture funds as Google Ventures or Kleiner Perkins. The founder, Doug Evans, imagined transposing the principle of the Nespresso coffee maker and capsules into the world of fruit and vegetable juices. His concept? Making healthful beverages in no time at all thanks to a powerful, expensive, connected machine squeezing pouches of pre-chopped fruit and vegetable with four tons of force—enough pressure, according to the startup's pitch, to lift two Teslas[1].

---

1. Lucie Ronfaut, "Juicero, la startup qui fait payer 400 dollars pour boire du jus de fruits," *Lefigaro.fr*, April 21, 2017.

These technological feats were meant to justify the high price of the invention developed by the Juicero teams: "After creating a high-tech product, the company initially set the price of its press at \$700, before lowering it to \$400 in early 2017. And each pack, good for a single glass of juice, was sold between \$5 and \$7[2]." With this supposedly revolutionary idea, Doug Evans believed he was riding the wave of food tech and dietary health. He even saw himself as the Steve Jobs of juice, crusading against unhealthy eating… Unfortunately, this dream came to an abrupt end in April 2017, after a Bloomberg News report with a video in which journalists demonstrated that the same result could be obtained by squeezing the packs by hand. A few months later, the startup closed down.

1. Product obsession, another facet of the technology mirage

The example of DEC

The history of Juicero is obviously an extreme example since the device was of no use to the consumer. But it remains also symbolic of a flaw that can be found in many companies: the tendency to overfocus on product and technology to the detriment of the coherence of the products and services offered. Danny Miller identified this mistake when he talked about companies that were "rigidly controlled, detail obsessed Tinkerers, firms whose insular, technocratic cultures alienate customers with perfect but irrelevant offerings[3]." This what the case, for instance, with Digital Equipment Corporation (DEC), IBM's main rival until the 1980s. Founded in 1957 by engineers from MIT, the company introduced an extremely

---

2. Jérôme Marin, "Juicero, la startup devenue la risée de la Silicon Valley, ferme ses portes," *Lemonde.fr*, September 2, 2017.

3. Danny Miller, *op. cit.*

reliable minicomputer with sophisticated hardware that proved quite popular with manufacturers.

A model of efficiency, the company began to decline when the market for PCs experienced a sharp downturn. Management had not anticipated this development, because the company culture was not very marketing-minded and not particularly sensitive to the emergence of new consumer behaviors. When DEC finally entered the office automation business, it continued to use the same methods that until then had attracted their B2B customers. Unfortunately, this failed because the company "failed to adapt its marketing and sales strategies to the new, less computer-friendly customers it encountered, DEC's products and manuals alike required an unrealistic amount of computer literacy" so they appeared to have been developed to appeal to engineers rather than to please the general public[4].

DEC cofounder and president Ken Olson was known for his aversion to marketing and communication. During the 1983 Super Bowl, he is said to have told his executives that "one minute of advertising in that game would pay for 600,000 handbooks," a remark typical of his technocentric approach. Several marketers then left the company in frustration[5]. The anecdote seems all the more ironic in that, Apple used advertising brilliantly during the Super Bowl the following year, in a commercial introducing the Macintosh computer[6]. While DEC was slowly declining, trapped in its operating modes and engineering issues, Steve Jobs was reinventing the codes of computer marketing.

Product obsession exists both in the way some startups position themselves and in large companies convinced their invention ticks all the boxes and meets market expectations, and believing that is sufficient to trigger the buying process.

---

4. *Ibid.*

5. *Ibid.*

6. See Chapter III.

If investors spent more than \$100 million on Juicero, it is because in theory, its machine presented all the characteristics likely to seduce a large clientele and conquer a growing fresh juice market in the United States: a Nespresso capsule's simplicity of use, an iPhone's sleek design, a business model based on subscription and renewal[7]. But ultimately these ingredients didn't work. What Juicero was missing more than anything else was a relevant offer—and a minimum of attention to marketing basics. Even in the age of *junk tech*, it is difficult to fool consumers with a product and price that is uncorrelated to any need. And what's more, invention is not synonymous with innovation[8].

Going beyond the product: the search
for a relevant offering

This is a lesson that Pazzi, a French startup that created a pizza robot capable of making 100 pizzas per hour with a repertoire of 5 million different recipes, will have to keep in mind. On paper, the product looks interesting: for example, it will make it possible to open fully automated and autonomous restaurants in train stations, airports, shopping malls and other places people pass through, where—in addition to the spectacle of the machine itself—customers will be able to enjoy fast, top-quality food at any time of day or night. Although Pazzi's technology seems promising, this alone will not guarantee its success. To realize its full potential, the company will need to develop a comprehensive offering that resonates with consumers' desires and the B2B clients to whom it will be licensed. Even if the product is perfect, reliable and fast, even if it allows people to become much more efficient, those qualities will not be determining factors in making the product addictive and standing out in the fast

---

7. Lucie Ronfaut, *op. cit.*

8. For more information on this, see Chapter V.

food market; it is also necessary to be wary of the technology mirage, and to make concentrated efforts on strategic marketing[9].

Making the leap from a good product (or even a bad one) and a relevant offering usually requires turning and repositioning. As Nespresso's trajectory demonstrates, it is essential to take into account all aspects of marketing if you want to create a kind of customer addiction. Before it became a brand with global reach and a level of profitability comparable to that of the luxury industry, Nespresso had long been groping for a sustainable business model. It took more than twenty years for the technology patented by a Nestlé engineer to become a commercial success.

Initially proposed to hotel and restaurant professionals, at first the product did not convince many users. Nespresso's tour de force was then to have conquered the general public by "combining technological innovation with immaterial innovation, enabling it to meet both a tangible need—that of a small black coffee one could find just around the corner—and a psychological expectation of sophistication, rarity, exclusivity[10]." The company's entire marketing strategy has been oriented towards this objective: giving customers—referred to as Nespresso Club members—the feeling that they are experiencing something extraordinary, that they are part of an exceptional community. This is one way to satisfy narcissism in today's world. From price to distribution channels via advertising campaigns and packaging, everything was designed to serve this ambition. Nespresso built a coherent offer in which all dimensions reinforce one another, putting the company's raison d'être into perspective. The product itself—a cup of coffee that is "hard to get hold of, almost

---

9. For more information on this, see Chapter I.

10. Caroline Castets, "Nespresso, bienvenue au club," *Lenouveleconomistes.fr*, July 7, 2011.

impossible to recyclable and extremely expensive[11]"—has almost taken a back seat.

2. The quest for "fit": from expanding your offering to maximizing value

A series of interdependent choices

"Fit" is an essential concept whose "role in strategy highlights yet another popular misconception, that competitive success can be explained by one core competence, the one thing you do really well. The fallacy here is that good strategies don't rely on just one thing, on making one choice. Nor do they typically result from even a series of independent choices. Good strategies depend on the connection among many things, on making interdependent choices[12]," including the fundamentals of the marketing mix (*Product, Price, Place, Promotion*[13]) to which new criteria (Packaging, Presence, Positioning, Purpose[14]) can now be added. In this case, the saying "The best ad is a good product[15]" does not actually hold true. It may have been valid in a consumer society dominated by the culture of efficiency, but it is no longer persuasive in the aspirational age, as seen in the example of DEC.

Groups such as Ikea and Zara are frequently cited as exemplars of fit. All the elements of their value proposition are

---

11. *Ibid.*

12. Joan Magretta, *Understanding Michael Porter: The Essential Guide to Competition and Strategy*. Harvard Business Press, December 2011.

13. These are the 4Ps, the marketing mix concept from the 1960s and taught for years in business schools: *product, price, place, promotion*. This approach has gradually been replaced by models centered on the customer and the "4Cs": consumer, cost, convenience and communication.

14. The raison d'être overlaps with the company's primary objective and what is called a sense of purpose.

15. Quote attributed to American academic Alan Meyer.

interdependent and interrelated and give them a competitive advantage. As heirs to industries where cost reduction is a categorical imperative, these companies have been able to transform this constraint into an asset. The Swedish home furnishings store was one of the first to focus on every aspect of the customer experience and to concentrate its energy on lifestyle of the middle-class: no-frills furniture design, low prices, warehouses attached to stores, car-friendly locations and ample free parking, flat packs to simplify transportation, decorated full-room product displays, in-store cafeterias and boutiques with Swedish products, a logo in the colors of the mother country, a shopping trail that looks like a Scandinavian getaway, etc. Taken separately, none of the links in the value chain offers real superiority; together, they enhance one another. Their cumulative impact forms a particularly effective whole[16].

The sanctification of speed and availability

As far as Zara is concerned, the fashion retailer has made speed and "fast fashion" its trademark and ideological heart. "At every step in the value chain, Zara has configured its activities so that nothing takes longer than it needs to: its design teams are configured for rapid response; its plants are located nearby; its own fleet of trucks ensures rapid delivery; its investments in IT speed communications between design and manufacturing. Each activity contributes[17]" to this goal, and to the satisfaction of a clientele whose tastes are constantly evolving.

In a world of immediacy and volatility of uses, the quest for speed and availability have become essential components of the offering. This is what Amazon promises its clients: an infinite number of products that can be found in one click and delivered in record time. In spite of their good public image and territorial coverage, brands such as Fnac Darty

---

16. Joan Magretta, *op. cit.*
17. *Ibid.*

(the French electrical retail company) have had great difficulty competing with Jeff Bezos' company. Despite efforts to improve delivery times and diversify shopping methods, they still represent a world where product knowledge and the sales force's technological expertise were the main criteria for consumer choice. Although some individuals are still attached to this added value, it is no longer the central aspiration of our time. A physical point of sale is only important if it brings something extra, something that serves the overall offer and the company's purpose. This is a critical issue for all companies in distribution and e-commerce: renewing their positioning and existing in a market in which a handful of giants (Amazon, Alibaba) are tapping into the zeitgeist and shaping consumer behavior. Brands such as Amazon have not only met our expectations and our desire to own "everything right now." They have made us addicted to speed and directly contributed to the acceleration of our lifestyles.

Amazon's talent also lies in its early integration of third-party vendors into its marketplace to expand its product range and meet availability requirements: in 2018, 58 percent of merchandise sold on Amazon came from third-party vendors, compared to 3 percent in 1999. This is a novel approach to marketing by treating potential competitors as customers. Abolishing the distinction between players and freeing oneself from traditional market considerations are gradually becoming the norm. AWS therefore provides Netflix with its cloud computing services, while Jeff Bezos' group is in direct competition with the streaming platform in the production and distribution of content (Amazon Prime Video, Amazon Studios). This entanglement is linked to the evolution of marketing and the breaking down of borders between different sectors of the economy[18]: Amazon is all at once a retailer, a cloud provider and an entertainment business.

―――――――――――

18. Casino, the French supermarket chain, adopted a similar approach with GreenYellow, its subsidiary specializing in green energy. Founded

To establish itself in the audiovisual landscape, Netflix has also emphasized the coherence of its offer. With identical products—films and series in a 52-minute format—the streaming platform has succeeded in supplanting most of the historical leaders in the sector. In France, Netflix now has more subscribers than Canal Plus, the premium television channel[19]. Many specialists explain that Netflix's success is based on algorithms, data and the ability to shape and promote programs according to the viewer's tastes. This is undoubtedly an important factor, even more so if we refer to the program classification system it uses; in addition to traditional categories (youth, humor, horror, etc.), Netflix addresses specific communities ("LGBTQ," "Girls' Night In," "Children and Family Watch Together," "Teen TV"), leaving little doubt about the profiling and targeting of users, who are offered content that is meant to reflect their intimate concerns and appeal to their narcissism. Conscious of the sense of mystery surrounding its algorithms, the platform has relied heavily on this image to gain popularity and forge its legend. Modeled after Coca-Cola's secret formula, Netflix has hinted that it possesses a magical ingredient, plucked from the depths of data, enabling it to produce successful series such as *House of Cards*. But this is more marketing strategy than reality[20].

---

in 2007 within the Casino group, over time GreenYellow's energy-efficiency services have been marketed to other industries and retailers endeavoring to improve the energy efficiency of their buildings and reduce their carbon footprint. As with AWS (Amazon Web Services), here a solution designed for internal use found natural outlets on the market. Again, "porosity" is the key.

19. François Bougon, "Salto, l'anti-Netflix de France TV, TF1 et M6, est annoncé pour 2020," *Lemonde.fr*, August 13, 2019.

20. "Netflix supposedly possesses an algorithm that allows them to produce content viewers are sure to like. This is how the legend of *House of Cards* was born. The series is said to be the result of Netflix's ultra-secret algorithm. This 'information' was widely relayed - even by many journalists specializing in cinema - and is more like an urban legend or a plot out of *Minority Report*..." Paul Vacca, "Hollywood, la Silicon Valley et nous," *Medium.com*, December 2, 2016.

The technological argument is not the only one that comes into play. In order to distinguish itself from the competition, Netflix has focused from the outset on consumption of on-demand content via a digital platform, and a pay-per-view subscription system that provides flexibility at all levels (medium, time, place) and makes it possible to reach a new audience that includes "cord nevers" (people who have never paid for a traditional TV connection and use Internet to stream content), "cord cutters" (people who cancel their subscription to cable and pay television channels and switch to video on demand) and "cord shavers" (people switching to the least expensive subscription package)[21]. This is not a simple change in the channel of diffusion: it is part of the revolution in speed and availability. In addition, it creates product addiction in viewers 2.0 who no longer have to wait a week to watch their favorite show. Although it no longer provides information on this point, the channel has long boasted that it is conducive to binge watching, the practice of watching multiple episodes of a television program in rapid succession[22]. At a time when audience attention is a scarce resource[23] and is the object of a fierce battle between audiovisual and digital players, Netflix is giving itself the means to keep them in its bosom by breaking with the temporality that until now has governed the broadcasting of series: "This is no longer an 'impulsive addiction' linked to tension or repetition as in linear TV—with cliffhangers and twists distributed arithmetically throughout the season to structure interest—but a new kind of 'addiction to flow': immersive and profound. The rhythmic addiction

---

21. *Ibid.*

22. See for instance on the streaming platform's website: "Netflix & Binge: New Binge Scale Reveals TV Series We Devour and Those We Savor," *netflix.com*, June 8, 2016, https://about.netflix.com/en/news/netflix-binge-new-binge-scale-reveals-tv-series-we-devour-and-those-we-savor-1

23. Michael D. Smith, Rahul Telang, "Data Can Enhance Creative Projects—Just Look at Netflix," *Hbrfrance.fr*, January 23, 2018.

of the old-fashioned series is being succeeded by a kind of arrhythmic addiction[24]." The French broadcasting companies (France Télévisions, TF1 and M6), which in response recently created a new streaming service, Salto, will have to reflect on this issue. Building viewer loyalty is not just a question of content[25]—Canal Plus proposes excellent television series, and TF1 remains an expert in entertainment—but of the offer itself. Creating a common platform with good programs will serve no purpose if these broadcasters do not work more on anticipating the audience's habits and aspirations. For the moment, they are moving forward with one or more delays.

Arbitration of priorities and coherence: a balancing act

But building a coherent offering is not an easy process. Like large companies confronted with "the innovator's dilemma," the vast majority of organizations are torn between optimizing their business model for their customers and adopting disruptive new technologies to enhance their aspirational dimension. Even players in the new economy and the digital world are forced to control costs and to respect certain efficiency constraints, which sometimes conflicts with the desire to revolutionize the value chain and offer customers a new experience. Tesla recently learned the hard way when its founder, Elon Musk, announced the closure of all Tesla car dealerships and outlets and distribute its vehicles exclusively online, thereby lowering prices and reaching a wider customer base.

---

24. Paul Vacca, *op. cit.*

25. While video-on-demand (VOD) services are becoming more and more popular, it is worth noting that sports is the only content broadcast in real time that retains a strong addictive potential since it is based on the unknown and adrenaline. The success of the Twitch platform, on which gamers live-broadcasts video games and esports tournaments, is largely based on this principle.

This choice, which concerned only one link in the value chain, had immediate repercussions that cast doubt on Tesla's strategy. Given the sharp drop in prices, around $5,000 on high-end models, recent Tesla buyers felt cheated. A few days later, Elon Musk decided to backtrack, saying that some of Tesla's showrooms would remain open, which led to a slight increase in prices, but more importantly raised some fundamental questions: Can a car manufacturer do without physical outlets? Even if online shopping is progressing in this sector and extending the laws of digitalization to traditional industries, is it possible to switch to a 100 percent digital distribution model? Doesn't a customer who invests $100,000 in a vehicle want to test it before acquiring it? If Musk's intuition was relevant and went in the direction of current evolutions, implementing his ideas proved more difficult than expected, and Tesla is still looking for an adequate distribution model[26]. Elon Musk's turnarounds demonstrate the complexity of aligning all components of the offering and achieving perfect consistency. Even though the company reached a record $464 billion valuation in the summer of 2020, its model is still questionable and the volatility of its shares remains very high[27].

In a completely different vein, the French rap group PNL—two brothers known for their disruptive communication, keen marketing sense and scarcity in the media, which feeds their fans hunger for their music—disappointed some in June 2019, when they entered into an exclusive partnership with Apple Music to release four new songs: "the choice of an exclusive platform led here to the product's transition from a 'rare' status to that of 'accessible to the privileged,' and many fans, integrated into the community of values, felt betrayed, or at least sidelined. In this strategy of rarity, there is a need for

---

26. Sun Kim, "Tesla à la recherche de son modèle de distribution," *www.lesechos-etudes.fr*, March 15, 2019.

27. Guillaume Renouard, "Tesla, chronique d'une bulle boursière annoncée ?" *Latribune.fr*, September 7, 2020.

accessibility, especially when proximity is a parallel strategic dimension[28]." The search for the right balance can be perilous when you modify a component of your offering. A product that is adored by the public and supported by a close-knit community is never immune to these setbacks. For Tesla, as with PNL, a simple adjustment of the distribution channel led to unsuspected disruptions.

Sense of purpose and a company's primary goal

Nevertheless, there are a few simple rules to observe when you want to maximize the impact of your offering and value creation. Too many companies, especially young French and European startups, use their products as a starting point to describe their activity and the way they intend to implement it. This is striking when you listen to pitches by entrepreneurs knocking at the door of venture capital firms. An episode of the television series *Silicon Valley*, on the other hand, shows us, in a caricaturish tone, young California geeks who all claim to want "change the world" when they present their startup project[29]. It may seem a bit megalomaniacal or opaque, but it is the best way to address the aspirations of future clients.

Here we find the well-known theories of "start with why" and the "golden circle of innovation," both concepts created by Simon Sinek, leadership expert and professor at Columbia University: People don't buy what you do; they buy why you do it[30]. "Nike doesn't just sell sporting goods but promises consumers to excel and experience the pleasure of competition;

---

28. Tarik Chakor, Hugo Gaillard, "PNL, groupe de rap et cas d'école marketing," *Hbrfrance.fr*, July 17, 2019.

29. Jean-Baptiste Rudelle, *op. cit.*

30. Simon Sinek, *Start with Why. How Great Leaders Inspire Everyone to Take Action*, Portfolio/Penguin, December 2011; Simon Sinek, *Find Your Why. A Practical Guide for Discovering Purpose for You and Your Team*, Portfolio/Penguin, September 2017.

Walt Disney doesn't just offer cartoons and amusement parks but promises to make people happy; McKinsey doesn't just offer consulting services but promises businesses and governments to deliver success[31]." The French and Europeans, who take a more rational approach, often confuse this emphasis on "why" with a kind of "bullshit[32]."

The Lego Group was able to capitalize on this vein when it recorded financial losses in the late 1990s. In order to turn itself around, the famous Danish company stopped seeing itself as a manufacturer of plastic bricks and turned into a brand selling dreams to children. In particular, it entered into partnerships with franchises (*Harry Potter, Jurassic Park, Indiana Jones, Stranger Things…*) to sell its products in the world of cinema and video games. Lego also strengthened the emotional bond with its fans by encouraging them to take ownership of the brand and become ambassadors for the group, by encouraging them to invent their own models, by broadcasting content on social networks and by creating a community linked by the same passion. More generally, Lego took up ingredients that Apple had used to redefine the traditional 4Ps of business, Product, Place, Promotion, and Price: "Apple was the first company to understand a vastly changing consumer world where the old 4Ps were no longer viable. Many companies have tried to imitate it, mimicking an element of Apple's products such as its sleek designs or 'cool' advertising. But when competitors focus on just the superficial elements of competitiveness, they miss the entire 'ecosystem' of innovation that Apple created. Lego is second to Apple in understanding the transformation of the 4Ps. Their flair to set-up the same type of powerful ecosystem accounts for why Lego has become a stellar player in the toy market. What both Apple and Lego invented is effectively a

---

31. Jean-Michel Palagos, Julia Maris, *Diriger en ère de rupture. Brouillard et solitude*, Hermann, May 2016.

32. For more information on this, see Chapter VI.

new set of marketing success factors: Passion, Personalization, Periphery and Partnering[33]," markers more in line with the aspirational age.

In other words, a company will build a coherent offer all the more easily the more it has found a raison d'être and strengthened its sense of "purpose," a primary objective that will guide all the rest of its approach (the product, the price, the distribution channel, the communication, etc.). More than ever, it is necessary to start with "why" and question the finality of his value proposition. This approach is fundamental in order to exploit all the facets of its offer. In B2B, one of the solutions is to focus on the end customer (its client's "consumer" or user) and to contribute in this context to its business development, synonymous with growth.

Eficia, a startup supported by Aster Capital, a new growth accelerator, followed this path to give new impetus to its business model (often referred to as "pivoting" in entrepreneurial jargon). Originally called ECO GTB and specializing in "smart building," this company initially aimed to "optimize the energy and economic performance of buildings in real time" and to reduce the cost of energy consumption, in particular those generated by lighting and by heating and cooling. If the promise to reduce energy bills from 15 to 30 percent was obviously attractive to building managers, it lacked an aspirational dimension, and failed to align itself with the its customers' objectives, and thus to contribute to their growth. Taking a step back, the young company undertook an important iterative study and managed to free itself from its initial offer; it found a more coherent proposition for its customers with the possibility that buildings contribute to the company's development, like "virtual salespeople." How? Simply by

---

33. Estelle Métayer, "Comment Lego a réinventé les 4P du marketing," *Hbrfrance.fr*, December 19, 2014. English translated published online by the author https://www.linkedin.com/pulse/how-lego-re-invented-4ps-estelle-metayer

focusing more on the consumer's perceived comfort at the point of sale. The technical solution remained unchanged; only the building's management and orientation were altered to serve a more ambitious—and above all much more profitable—purpose for its customers. The offer met with immediate success from several retail brands such as Decathlon (a French sporting-goods company) or GiFi (a French business for decoration, furniture and gardening), which saw it as a way to improve customer experience and ultimately increase profits[34]. Eficia's vision thus shifted from the question of infrastructure to that of the use or occupancy of buildings, a change that has been synonymous with a qualitative leap. This ingenious solution now drives more than 2,000 buildings in Europe and is continuing its internationalization with a new dynamic far superior to the one it enjoyed when the company first started[35].

Here again, everything is a question of positioning. The same product or technology can give rise to diametrically opposed results depending on the importance managers give to marketing strategies and to their sense of purpose. Those with a "well-formed intellect[36]" have a hard time admitting it, but often the simplest solutions give rise to a coherent offer and condition a company's success.

---

34. As Eficia's founder, Alric Marc, points out, "in distribution, the success of customer experience depends in part on thermal comfort, which is an element at the heart of our strategy, and this explains why we have been present in this sector from the very beginning." Olivier Durand, "Eficia ou l'efficacité énergétique," <www.filiere-3e.fr>, 4 juillet 2019. As Eficia's founder, Alric Marc, points out, "in distribution, the success of customer experience depends in part on thermal comfort, which is an element at the heart of our strategy, and this explains why we have been present in this sector from the very beginning."

35. *Eficia.com.*

36. From *The Essays of Michel de Montaigne,* written in 1580. Montaigne wrote that a teacher should possess "a well-formed rather than a well-filled intellect" (in the original French, "*plutôt* la *tête bien faite* que *bien pleine*").

V.

Renouncing the Cult of Intellect.
"Keep it Simple Stupid!"

> Men are intelligent and imaginative;
> they look backwards and ahead; they
> invent ingenious explanation for obser-
> ved phenomena; they devise elaborate
> and roundabout means for the achieve-
> ment of remote ends. Their intelligence,
> which has made them the masters of
> the world, often causes them to act
> like imbeciles.
>
> Aldous Huxley,
> *Jesting Pilate: The Diary of a Journey*

Although the wheeled suitcase can be found among the innovations that have most simplified the lives of tourists and travelers in recent decades, it is not based on revolutionary technology. Its late arrival was the result of observation and intuition on the part of Bernard Sadow, vice president of a luggage company. On his way home from a family vacation in the Caribbean in 1970, while lugging his bags through the airport during a stopover in Puerto Rico, he noticed an airport employee pushing heavy machinery on a wheeled skid. This inspired him to replicate the idea on a small scale, and he fashioned a suitcase with wheels that would ease the burden for travelers and baggage handler.

After a period of repeated rejections, Bernard Sadow's invention was picked up by the Macy's department store in New York and patented in 1972, but met with limited success. The suitcases, initially pulled by a strap, proved impractical and not particularly ergonomic. It took another fifteen years for Robert Plath, an airline pilot, to invent a long, extendable handle, after which rolling luggage finally made its mark on the general public, invading train stations and airport terminals[1]. In short, we were able to fly an airplane and put a man on the moon before imagining something as simple as the wheeled suitcase[2]. This seems to defy rational analysis!

1. Don't confuse invention and innovation

Simplicity, common sense and chance: the foundations of innovation

Still, this kind of situation is a constant in the history of innovation: most breakthroughs are not based on inventions that are new and original; they emerge from simple, a priori obvious and sensible ideas that bring obsolete technologies up to date or modernize the way they are used. Accidents and luck can sometimes be determining factors in their emergence. The wheel may have existed since 3,500 B.C. and the luggage since at least the time of the Phoenicians, but no one had thought of combining these two transportation technologies until the 1970s.

---

1. Joe Sharkey, "Reinventing the Suitcase by Adding the Wheel," *Nytimes.com*, October 4, 2010, Jérôme Barthélémy, "Pourquoi des innovations évidentes tardives – l'exemple de la valise à roulettes," *Xerficanal. com*, November 22, 2015.

2. Nassim Nicholas Taleb, *Antifragile: Things That Gain From Disorder*, Random House, November 2012.

In addition, the vast majority of innovations that transform people's daily lives are not the result of theoretical or scientific models. They come from work by practitioners who have experimented with their findings, improved discoveries made by others, used the trial-and-error (now known as test and learn) method or corrected defects in previous inventions. As Nassim Nicolas Taleb, a former hedge-fund manager turned mathematician and philosopher, explains, citing examples from the evolution of medicine, cooking or the Industrial Revolution, "the simpler and more obvious the discovery, the less equipped we are to figure it out by complicated methods. The key is that the significant can only be revealed through practice[3]." Author of *The Black Swan*, Taleb adds, using his signature provocative style, "both governments and universities have done very, very little for innovation and discovery, precisely because, in addition to their blinding rationalism, they look for the complicated, the lurid, the newsworthy, the narrated, the scientistic, and the grandiose, rarely for the wheel on the suitcase. Simplicity, I realized, does not lead to laurels[4]."

Although his caustic allegation might have been more nuanced, it aptly highlights a recurring flaw among government decision-makers and business leaders. Indeed, the cult of intellect and the rejection of simplicity lead many to curb innovation by supporting solutions that are too sophisticated. We might also quote the fundamental principle of logic of *Les Shadoks,* a French animated television series: Why make things simple when you can make them complicated?

A variant of the culture of efficiency and product hypertrophy[5], this trap is further encouraged by frequent confusion about the difference between invention and innovation. While invention refers above all to the discovery of new technologies, innovation introduces the concept of *use* of

---

3. *Ibid.*
4. *Ibid.*
5. For more information on this, see Chapter IV.

an idea or invention[6]. To illustrate this, the steam engine is an excellent example. The Greeks designed an "operating version[7]" for their own amusement called an aeolipyle, made in the shape of a turbine that would spin when the water inside it was heated. It was designed by Heron of Alexandria, an engineer and mathematician who lived in the first century AD. But the Greeks never made any significant use of it. It was not until some 1,600 years later with the First Industrial Revolution that the process was reconsidered and became the basis for breakthrough innovations. As for the technique of the wheel, it was long believed to have been ignored by such civilizations as the Mayans and Zapotecs. In fact, the Mesoamericans were aware of the wheel but did not use it to transport the heavy loads and huge blocks of stone intended to build their pyramids, even though this would have made their task easier[8]. Their children's toys, however, were equipped with wheels[9]...

---

6. A professor of strategy and innovation, Frédéric Fréry aptly states that we "confuse [...] discovery and its diffusion. If invention consists of developing something that never before existed, innovation refers to its diffusion among the public. So long as a new product is a prototype confined to research laboratories, it is an invention. The day this invention becomes accessible—most often through commercialization—it becomes an innovation. [...] What concerns companies is innovation, not invention." Frédéric Fréry, "L'innovation, ce n'est pas l'invention," *Hbrfrance. fr*, November 3, 2014.

7. Nassim Nicholas Taleb, *op. cit.*

8. The lack of draft animals to pull carts and wagons explains in part why these civilizations did not think of using the wheel for practical purposes and convert it into a breakthrough innovation for transportation. However, they had had the intuition to do so, since they used wooden logs to roll the most massive loads.

9. Nassim Nicholas Taleb, *op. cit.*

Inventor or innovator: a vast difference

If indeed there is a gap between inventions and the specific achievements that result from them, it would be wrong to believe it is mainly a thing of the past. In this age of digital and technological proliferation, few people manage to transform invention into innovation. As Nassim Nicolas Taleb points out, "implementation does not necessarily proceed from invention. It, too, requires luck and circumstances […] Sometimes you need a visionary to figure out what to do with a discovery, a vision that he and only he can have. For instance, take the computer mouse, or what is called the graphical interface: it took Steve Jobs to put it on your desk, then laptop[10]"—which was more a matter of sensitivity to consumer behavior than a technical question. If Steve Jobs had confined himself to "geek" problems, he would never have had such an influence on our digital lives. In fact, the first serious project for the iPhone did not originate in Jobs' mind; it was Marc Porat, an engineer who had anticipated the advent of a connected society and wanted to create a successor to the personal computer, who imagined the Pocket Crystal[11] years earlier, in the late 1980s.

Head of General Magic—a software and electronics company that was a spinoff of Apple—Porat tried to launch a tactile smartphone. His attempt failed because neither the technology nor its uses had matured enough when the Pocket Crystal was first developed and marketed. The Pocket Crystal faced the same barriers as Apple's personal assistant, the Newton. But the concept was revived ten years later,

---

10. *Ibid.*

11. Marc Porat described the object as "a tiny computer, phone, a very personal object. It must be beautiful, […] It will offer the comfort of a touchstone, the tactile satisfaction of a seashell, the enchantment of a crystal. Once you use it you won't be able to live without it." Fabien Benoît, "L'entreprise qui inventa l'iPhone 20 ans avant Steve Jobs," *Usbek & Rica*, n° 27, July-August-September 2019.

in a different context and with renewed techniques, thanks to Steve Jobs, who completely revolutionized mobile telephony and the Internet[12]. Apple's founder may not have been an inventor, but he was an outstanding innovator.

Nowadays, we sometimes forget that "innovation is as much about entrepreneurs as it is about researchers. [...] Apple [...] has no in-house technology lab but has been able to innovate based on others' inventions. Before the Macintosh, there was the Xerox Star workstation, introduced in 1981. Before the iPhone, there was the Nokia Communicator, created in 1996. Before the iPad, there was the Microsoft Tablet PC, presented in 2000. But Apple innovated in other ways that led to market acceptance of these products on a completely different scale[13]." The teams of the American multinational focused on the uses and aspirations of people 2.0. France is fortunate to have a myriad of creative startups and large companies that are increasing the number of patent applications. According to data from the EPO (European Patent Office), in 2019, France was in place to rank second in Europe and fourth in the world, behind the United States, Germany and Japan but ahead of China and the United Kingdom[14]. These indicators are certainly encouraging, but they are not enough to make France innovative. For the moment, it remains a country of inventors. France is imagining new technologies, but it is not succeeding in creating real breakthroughs in existing markets and giving French Tech an aspirational aura. These figures should also be seen in perspective, since 40 percent of patents remain unexploited and only 1 patent out of 1,000 provides an offer that can generate exceptional profits[15].

---

12. *Ibid.*

13. Emmanuelle Duez, Marianne Urmès, "Ne confondons pas invention et innovation!," *Latribune.fr*, September 19, 2016.

14. Enrique Moreira, "Demandes de brevets : la France conserve le deuxième rang européen," *Lesechos.fr*, 12 mars 2019.

15. Frédéric Fréry, *op. cit.*

2. Too smart to succeed?

Creativity is not enough

While innovation should not be confused with invention, neither should it be reduced to creativity. Innovation and creativity are two complementary approaches that follow different methodologies and purposes. In reality, "innovation […] is a matter of management: it is about getting things done, making sure new ideas are not killed off by a company's organization, routines, budgetary constraints and power struggles, that they find their way onto the market. Of course, one has to ensure a flow of new ideas to irrigate the innovation process. But to confine oneself to creativity is to remain in theory, whereas innovation is a practice[16]." There is an element of risk inherent in the innovation process. It involves jumping into the deep end by testing one's product with customers, accepting failure and rectifying the situation as many times as necessary. Eric Ries, an entrepreneur and author of the bestseller *The Lean Startup*, says the same thing when he argues for ongoing improvement, greater speed and efficiency and continuous innovation[17]. Contrary to the kinds of luminous ideas that make it possible for you to shine in public, to give fine speeches and feel smarter, the innovation process involves a form of modesty and pragmatism. This does not prevent you from being ambitious and from shooting for the moon, but it does require you to remain anchored in reality.

With rare exceptions, the French, Europeans and a number of Americans from the East Coast are too smart to succeed in today's innovation ecosystem. Victims of the "Soviet-Harvard delusion" described by Nassim Nicolas Taleb, they believe

---

16. Frédéric Fréry, "L'innovation, ce n'est pas la créativité," *Hbrfrance.fr*, 27 octobre 2014.

17. Eric Ries, *The Lean Startup. How Constant Innovation Creates Radically Successful Businesses*, Portfolio Penguin, October 2011.

in the superiority of theory over practice, and this imprisons them in the trap of the "naive rationalist": they overestimate the reach of abstract scientific knowledge in human relationships or in developing their business, and they undervalue empirical knowledge based on a more intuitive, less codifiable approach[18]. In a technological galaxy shaped by dream peddlers and creators of product addicts, they continue to believe that it is the engineers, the Cartesian minds, that possess the essence of truth and power. But these attributes have changed hands. The techno-magicians have gradually replaced the technocrats of the old world.

The harmful consequences of naive rationalism

Naive rationalism and the cult of intellect have three harmful consequences for companies. First, they give rise to an aversion to failure and a weak culture regarding the right to make mistakes. In French companies in particular, these factors hinder innovation and the deployment of test and learn solutions[19]. Second, this psychological disposition fosters a feeling that risks and uncertainty can be neutralized by planning and forecasting models. Many large companies are committed to efficiency and "in love with the idea of the strategic plan. They need to pay to figure out where they are going. Yet there is no evidence that strategic planning works—we even seem to have evidence against it[20]," in the sense that it limits room for maneuvering and makes them less sensitive to unexpected market opportunities.

This deficiency also involves the world of European venture capital: most projects are evaluated in keeping with complex

---

18. Nassim Nicholas Taleb, *op. cit.*

19. Julien Cusin, "Vers l'instauration d'une culture du "droit à l'erreur" dans les entreprises innovantes," *Annales des Mines – Gérer et Comprendre,* 2011/2.

20. Nassim Nicholas Taleb, *op. cit.*

research that guarantees a startup's seriousness and future but also keeps them "locked up in a bureaucratic mold[21]" that is not particularly conducive to capturing the opportunities that may arise. Several empirical studies, notably those of Steven Shapin, a historian and sociologist of science, have shown that investors in Silicon Valley prefer to make decisions based on an entrepreneur's personality and passion rather than on seemingly more rational criteria (such as the specific ideas being pitched and the team's technical skills, for instance). Missionaries driven by entrepreneurial faith and the desire to change the world inspire more confidence than clerics who prudently follow the rules they learned in school. A 2016 survey of venture capital firms in the Silicon Valley region found that almost 50 percent based their decisions on intuition, and that 17 percent of original investors referred to no financial measures whatsoever when betting on a project. They considered that conventional wisdom would only lead to conventional returns and that a small dose of madness is needed in identifying the unicorn firms of tomorrow[22].

Third, naive rationalism and the cult of intellect lead to the rejection of simplicity, as if the latter were devoid of value and synonymous with stupidity. Following this logic, some managers refuse to admit the importance of marketing and reduce it either to a subordinate function or to a gimmick: an activity that does not deserve the attention of top management because it is not intellectually noble enough. Others are mistakenly convinced that by making processes, products or strategic orientations more complex, they will strengthen their company's positions… As

---

21. *Ibid.*

22. Steven Shapin, *The Scientific Life. A Moral History of a Late Modern Vocation*, University of Chicago Press, October 2008; Stuart Hogarth, "Valley of the unicorns: consumer genomics, venture capital and digital disruption," *New Genetics and Society. Critical Studies of Contemporary Biosciences*, n° 36, 2017; *Hbrfrance.fr*, May-June 2017, "How Venture Capitalists Really Assess a Pitch."

John Flannery, Jeff Immelt's short-lived successor as head of GE, acknowledged, "Complexity has hurt us"— on the contrary, it was complexity that harmed the group and weakened its value proposition[23]. There may have been more obvious and effective ways to run an initiative such as Predix, but the company missed its opportunity by underestimating the importance of marketing and by applying efficiency standards to digital issues. The management team was too smart to successfully lead the multinational's digital transformation[24].

3. Simplifying our lives or making them poorer?

A friction-free existence

Simplicity has virtues that we can no longer ignore. We have moved into a world in which simplification is used as a weapon of mass seduction for consumers. Digital platforms linking customers and sellers (a two-sided market) are extremely popular, first because they are have embraced this basic shift. Most people want to limit transaction costs, save time and escape the inconvenience linked to obtaining a product or service. These ingredients are the key to the success of Airbnb, for example: easy communication between travelers and their hosts, an intuitive search system and secure, simplified transactions between both parties[25].

In order for a platform to be adopted by the public and reach critical mass, it is essential that they allow people to enter and use them without friction. According to Geoffrey Parker, Marshall

---

23. Drake Bennett, "*How GE Went From American Icon to Astonishing Mess,*" *Bloomberg.com*, February 1, 2018.

24. For more information on this, see Chapter i.

25. Laure Claire Reillier, Benoît Reillier, *Platform Strategy: How to unlock the power of communities and networks to grow your business*, Routledge, May 2017.

Van Alstyne, and Sangeet Paul Choudary, the platform business is an inversion of a firm's concerns and functions: it must use its external activities to orchestrate its internal operations and strategy. Marketing becomes a central element that drives the deployment of digital technologies. Digital technologies are no longer just a means to serve the customer's aspirations and an offer that integrates from its conception the desire to live a fluid experience[26]. A platform that is too complex is doomed to failure. In the twenty-first century, Narcissus wants all aspects of existence to be simplified.

PayPal has been a pioneering company in this field. To reduce friction, the platform avoided discouraging users with endless verification procedures by asking only for an email address and a credit card to set up an account. This simple means of payment was accessible in a matter of minutes, in direct contrast with other sites. At the same time, PayPal introduced financial incentives not only to acquire new users but also to build user loyalty, increase user commitment and encourage users to recommend the platform to others. Thanks to the growing popularity of its payment system on eBay, PayPal was able to increasingly attract eBay's online sellers, who saw it as an excellent way to speed up transactions. Rather than spending huge amounts of money on traditional communication and advertisements, the company focused on a marketing strategy to make its users increasingly active and become ambassadors for the platform[27].

FinTech continues to move in this direction. Digital banks that compete with the traditional players in the sector have not invented breathtaking products to attract customers. Instead, they have simply targeted and segmented their offerings better while providing more comfort and flexibility to their users.

---

26. Geoffrey G. Parker, Marshall W. Van Alstyne, Sangeet Paul Choudary, *Platform Revolution. How Networked Markets Are Transforming the Economy and How to Make Them Work for You*, WW Norton & Co, August 2017.
27. *Ibid.*

To address millennials, the neobanks N26 and Revolut freed themselves from physical networks and chose digital marketing, focusing on the social networks and their brands' community aspect. By placing "user experience at the center of the game[28]" and sticking to the habits of the younger generation, they dusted off the image of banks that suffer from the poor quality of their web applications, the slowness of their procedures and the shortcomings of their online services. The bank advisor, associated with a source of hassle, is disappearing in favor of intuitive and ergonomic functionalities.

Insurtech companies (such as Alan, Luko or Lemonade), which strive to simplify their clients' lives while promising to reduce their bills, have also followed this logic, have strongly emphasized their aspirational dimension[29]. Lemonade, a New York-based startup valued at more than $3 billion when it went public in July 2020 and moved to France in September that same year, relies on a promise of redistribution and B-Corp certification to highlight its value proposition and its participation in the collective interest. This is a good way of mixing seemingly contradictory requirements: satisfying narcissistic consumers who want to free themselves of constraints by maximizing profit, and pleasing socially conscious citizens who want to reward virtuous organizations.

The stranglehold of invisible technology?

This movement has only just begun and will continue to grow in the years to come: the technologies that are being imposed on a large scale are those that blend into our daily lives and give us the feeling that we are getting rid of complexity, daunting tasks and everything that hinders our individual development. Here, as elsewhere, our narcissism plays a decisive role.

---

28. Edouard Lederer, "Les 4 clefs du succès pour les néobanques," *Lesechos.fr*, July 22, 2019.

29. For more information on this, see Chapter VI.

Broadly speaking, we can distinguish three phases in the history of the perceptions surrounding the development of information and communication technologies from the middle of the twentieth century. Until recently, from the end of the Second World War to the early 1990s, the apogee of the consumer society, we consented to these devices dominating and surpassing us. The engineer and the computer scientist were always figures of authority—as were the priest and the teacher in the past—symbols of the march of progress and holders of an expertise inaccessible to the common man. High-tech products were rare and expensive objects, comparable to those offered by the luxury goods industry. Owning a television or a video recorder with a host of parameters or options whose usefulness was unknown was almost a distinctive sign, an emblem of social and material ease. In the 1980s, having a personal computer was reserved for aficionados and the "chosen few" who could penetrate the mysteries of computing.

With the democratization of these tools and the work of pioneering organizations like Apple, our relationship to these objects has changed. Some companies have understood that we need to work on interactions and focus on "design thinking" to meet the desires of consumers concerned that technology adapts to them and not the other way around. From the 1990s to today, as people have become more familiar with the new IT developments, we have paradoxically witnessed a collapse in the technological good will: winning companies are those that have managed to hide the complexity of these devices. Over the last three decades, individuals have felt that they have become more self-reliant and more capable as a result of new technologies. By becoming computer literate and exploring the endless territory of the web, they have felt smarter and more powerful. Lulled by the sweet music of empowerment marketing, grasshoppers 2.0 has satiated their egos and quenched their thirst for unconstrained experiences.

Today, we are probably entering a third phase of collective representations. Our era is torn between fascination for the promises of the fourth industrial revolution and fear of losing control over innovations futures: the increasing interference of digital devices in our private lives, the lack of transparency of the GAFA, the emergence of new addictions and fantasies around singularity raise the specter of a technical takeover of our individual and collective future. These are not new concerns. These concerns reactivate old discussions and the fear that the looming "tide of technological revolution" could "so captivate, bewitch, dazzle, and beguile man[30]" to the point of putting him in a straitjacket and depriving him of his reflective faculties. This book does not pretend to participate in the philosophical debate on technology's influence on people and societies[31]. On the other hand, it seems clear that the narcissistic tendencies exalted by *junk tech* work against our free will and our judgment.

The error is probably analyzing these evolutions solely through the prism of technology, when technology is only a facilitator and gas pedal of deeper societal transformations. The strength of Silicon Valley companies and the promoters of *junk tech* is that they have been able to capture the spirit of the times to build myths that embrace and guide the aspirations of each and every one of us. Where the French and Europeans remain dependent on rational approaches, these organizations have become masters in the art of fabricating narratives that capture the public's attention.

---

30. Martin Heidegger, *Essais et conférences*, Gallimard, 1958; *Discourse on Thinking*, Harper & Row, 1966. Cited by Nicholas Carr, *"Is Google Making Us Stupid?"*; *The Shallows: What the Internet Is Doing to Our Brains* W. W. Norton & Company, June 2011.

31. There are two main schools of thought on this subject. For advocates of "technological determinism," technological progress, "which they see as an autonomous force outside man's control, has been the primary factor influencing the course of human history [...] At the other end of the spectrum are the instrumentalists [...] who [...] downplay the power of technology, believing tools to be neutral artifacts, entirely subservient to the conscious wishes of their users. Our instruments are the means we use to achieve our ends; they have no ends of their own." Nicholas Carr, *op. cit.*

VI.

FIGHTING DEPENDENCY ON A RATIONAL APPROACH. THE POWER OF NARRATIVE

> "Fiction isn't bad. It is vital. Without commonly accepted stories about things like money, states or corporations, no complex human society can function. We can't play football unless everyone believes in the same made-up rules, and we can't enjoy the benefits of markets and courts without similar make-believe stories."
>
> YUVAL NOAH HARARI,
> *Homo Deus. A Brief History of the Future*

In *Winning the Story Wars*, American author and entrepreneur Jonah Sachs explains that contemporary societies tend to confuse myths with lies or wild stories from the distant past. Imbued with Cartesianism, we have rejected symbolic thinking on the side of superstition[1]. We have forgotten the unifying function that myths and epics used to have. They act as a

---

1. Jonah Sachs, *op. cit.*

"glue" that binds individuals together to form communities[2]; they create links connecting individuals around shared beliefs. Convinced that these illusions, which were followed by the reign of science, technology and reason, had been removed from our analysis grid, we underestimate the presence of myths in our imagination and our daily environment, while at the same time we overestimate our rationality and intellectual discernment.

1. FORGING A COMPELLING STORY

The art of narration: a key to political and ideological confrontations

As the economist and philosopher Friedrich Hayek rightly pointed out, "An age of superstition is a time when people imagine they know more than they do. In this sense, the twentieth century was certainly an outstanding age of superstition, and the cause of this is an overestimation of what science has achieved[3]." The beginning of twenty-first century, which gives inordinate importance to the technological factor and neglects other driving forces, remains consistent with this observation. In reality, we are evolving in a digital civilization permeated by myths. In our mental environment, storytellers, shamans and other religious figures have been replaced by marketing specialists and CEOs who have become virtuosos in the art of storytelling[4]. The comparative advantage of Silicon Valley and the champions of *junk tech* lies largely in harnessing this power.

In many ways, the political field verifies this rule. The British essayist and professor Alex Evans, who analyzed the victory of

---

2. Yuval Noah Harari, *Sapiens: A Brief History of Humankind*, Vintage, April 2015.

3. Cited by Pierre-André Taguieff, *Le sens du progrès. Une approche historique et philosophique*, Flammarion, April 2004.

4. Jonah Sachs, *op. cit.*

Brexit and Donald Trump, borrowed the concept of "the myth gap" from Jonah Sachs to decipher the rise of populism and the debacle of centrist forces. According to him, the supporters of "Remain" and Hillary Clinton neglected the power of narrative in favor of technocratic and factual arguments that could not engage voters[5]. This does not mean that they should have used lies or spurious arguments to win. What they really lacked was the ability to give "direction"—in the sense of both guidance or motivating force and the position towards which someone moves—to their campaigns. Their project lacked a singular purpose.

In contrast, such personalities as Donald Trump know how to use this weapon. Whether some consider the former president of the United States to be stupid or dangerous changes nothing: his success is founded on a simple story (the outsider challenging the establishment), transgressive rhetoric that breaks with traditional codes, the designation of enemies (Washington elites, mass immigration) and a clear objective ("Make America Great Again," playing on the idea of a golden age). From a narrative point of view, Trump offered voters a coherent vision. Buoyed by the social networks and the individualization of propaganda messages on the Internet, his strategy mobilized large crowds, not only in physical gatherings but also virtually. This awakened America from its torpor, an America that no longer believed in political discourse. Donald Trump's election potion was not a souped-up version of populist opium but rather a cocktail of amphetamines calculated to hysterize his followers—a variant of *junk tech* used for political jousting[6]…

––––––––––––

5. Alex Evans, *The Myth Gap. What Happens When Evidence and Arguments Aren't Enough*, Eden Project Book, January 2017.

6. "Trump became stronger by supercharging individual agency, taking the reins off and championing unorthodox, previously socially unacceptable behaviors. His drug of choice is not one that subdues the populace, but one that excites it." Jeremy Heimans, Henry Timms, *New Power: How Power Works in Our Hyperconnected World—And How to Make It Work for You*, Anchor Books, 2019.

Alex Evans similarly explains that for a long time, political advocates of ecology struggled to make their voices heard because they presented the harms of carbon emissions and the opportunities of the energy transition in a way that was too rational and disembodied. But once they rewrote the same narrative but with a more dramatic tone (the risk of extinction of the human species), connecting it to moral ambition (the preservation of biodiversity and the fate of future generations) and an intelligible goal (keeping global warming under two degrees Celsius), they increased their audience and changed public opinion. They also changed the narrative by defining an enemy that needed to be fought (the oil and gas companies), playing the role of a kind of "big bad wolf" without whom the story would be less emotionally engaging[7]. In a way, Greta Thunberg's arrival in the media landscape radicalizes this approach. She embodies simultaneously the archetypal figure of a young woman predicting great misfortune (Cassandra), endowed with the status of the prophetess (Pythia) or chosen one (Rey Skywalker in *Star Wars*), ready to challenge those in power (Katniss Everdeen in *The Hunger Games*) and restore planetary balance by leading adults along the path of truth. The admiration and criticism she inspires go beyond reason; we are in the presence of a character who fits perfectly with the stories told by collapsologists.

A CEO's fundamental mission: to be an aspirational leader

Seen from this perspective, it is not surprising that the companies that fuel passions and create addiction are those that also build or regenerate mythologies in keeping with individual and collective aspirations. "Companies that inspire, companies that command trust and loyalty over the long term, are the ones that make us feel we're accomplishing something

---

7. *Ibid.*

bigger than just saving a buck," something that espouses a higher purpose[8]. The clients of these companies feel less like consumers than like privileged users or club members earning more value than they pay for. Take Apple as an example. This brand probably does not market smartphones that offer the best value for the money, and no evidence suggests that its technology outperforms the competition. Harvard professor Clayton M. Christensen famously predicted on two occasions, in 2007 and 2012, that the smartphone would not succeed[9]… which proves that most predictions, even when they are made by experts, have a low degree of reliability. Nevertheless, consumers who choose Apple are firmly convinced that they have access to an matchless experience, that they are joining a community of the happy few freed from the burdens of technological complexity by the ergonomics and creative genius of Steve Jobs' firm. This is the philosophy of "Think different." Great leaders fulfill a crucial mission in this respect. It is their job to give meaning and ideological heart to their company. In the aspirational age, the qualities of a great CEO are at least threefold— the right kind of ambition, the ability to articulate a vision, and the ability to achieve that vision by aligning the interests of employees with those of customers[10]. The leaders' role is to define their company's raison d'être: to benefit customers and society as a whole; to capture the fantasies, thoughts and dreams of the collective unconscious; to explore the territories of desire; to be able to convert them into a coherent offer. CEOs should embody not so much the company as the world of the client and the social utility of

---

8. Simon Sinek, *Find Your Why, op. cit.*

9. Bernard Buisson, Nabyla Daidj, "La disruption, obsession stérile des grandes entreprises," *Hbrfrance.fr*, March 21, 2017.

10. These three qualities are notably mentioned by the investor and entrepreneur Ben Horowitz in his book *The Hard Thing About Hard Things. Building a Business When There Are No Easy Answers*, Harper Business, March 2014.

their organization. They are not there to defend a brand but to act as "a mouthpiece" whose message permeates the entire company's ecosystem[11].

Elon Musk offers a perfect archetype of the "aspirational leader." According to his biographer, Ashlee Vance, he "speaks about the cars, solar panels, and batteries with such passion that it's easy to forget they are more or less sideline projects. He believes in the technologies to the extent that he thinks they're the right things to pursue for the betterment of mankind[12]." All his speeches and interventions are oriented to give meaning to the mission of the companies he manages (Tesla, Space X, SolarCity) and to their fundamental role for the survival of globe: the Earth free from the threat of global warming, free from the imminent flood, free from fossil fuels and thus conquering Mars to take a new civilizational step. His commitment to OpenAI, a company working for artificial intelligence with a human face, comes from the same ambition: to ward off the specter of a super-intelligence that could eventually destroy humanity. Like other Silicon Valley bosses, Elon Musk poses as the savior and the Noah[13] of modern times. Inspired by the world of superheroes and Marvel comics such as *Iron Man*[14], he creates a communication strategy and a

---

11. Theodore Kinni, "Sheryl Sandberg: Develop Your Voice, Not Your Brand," <www.gsb.stanford.edu>, July 17, 2017.

12. Ashlee Vance, *Elon Musk: Tesla, SpaceX, and the Quest for a Fantastic Future*, HarperCollins, 2015

13. "It is striking, moreover, that the film of the same name (*Noah*, directed by Darren Atonofsky), which stages the biblical story, the first opus of the post-apocalyptic genre, and the film *Interstellar*, which tells of humanity's great departure to another Earth, were released in theaters in the same year, 2014. [...] The 'survivalist' currents have never [...] flourished so greatly and show the entry of humanity as a kind of permanent millenarianism." Pierre-Henri d'Argenson, *La fin du monde et le dernier dieu. Un nouvel horizon pour l'humanité*, Liber, August 2018.

14. The reference to Iron Man and Jarvis, the AI system that powers his armor, was also taken up by Mark Zuckerberg to describe the virtual personal assistant he dreamed up for his home: "I'm going to start by

narrative that resonate with contemporary mythology while recycling the dreams (the conquest of space) that have always fascinated us.

2. VISION OR BULLSHIT? A FINE LINE

Fake it till you make it

In the orchestration of aspirations and myths, the trick is to place the cursor in the right place. The example of Elon Musk is interesting in that it is not clear if his companies are based on a sustainable business model or if they will eventually explode in flight. Tesla's performance and its ability to keep up with the industrial pace often seem unsure[15]: SpaceX developed inventive solutions for recycling rockets, but its plans to fly to the Moon and Mars has left some reviewers skeptical[16], and as for SolarCity, it lost its place as Number 1 in the sale of residential solar panels in the United States[17]. But Elon Musk continues to build up his list of spectacular promises: deploying a fleet of 1 million robotaxis, implanting a computer-interface system in the human brain using AI (Neuralink project), creating a Hyperloop tunnel that would zip people from Washington

----

exploring what technology is already out there. Then I'll start teaching it to understand my voice to control everything in our home—music, lights, temperature and so on. I'll teach it to let friends in by looking at their faces when they ring the doorbell. I'll teach it to let me know if anything is going on in [my daughter] Max's room that I need to check on when I'm not with her." Eric Sadin, *op. cit.*

15. Nabil Bourassi, "Tesla : les doutes font plonger le titre, mais les marchés financent la dette," *Latribune.fr*, May 24, 2019.

16. Julien Lausson, "SpaceX sur la Lune fin 2021 ? La NASA en doute," *Numerama.com*, July 29 2019.

17. Claude Fouquet, "Tesla propose désormais de louer sans engagement des panneaux solaires," *Lesechos.fr*, August 20, 2019.

to Baltimore in less than a half hour, and so on. [18]. In the United States, many observers wonder whether his grandiose statements mask a kind of "bullshit" that could jeopardize his companies' financial health[19]. In a way, this headlong rush, this flurry of astonishing announcements recalls Peter Thiel's warning for leaders in *From Zero to One*: "The greatest danger for a founder is to become too sure of his myth to the point of losing its common sense. But for a company, the other no less insidious danger would be to lose all sense of myth and to mistake disenchantment for wisdom[20]." The balance is not so easy to find.

One of the risks is the formation of a new bubble for tech startup whose valuation reaches exorbitant levels. This theory about Silicon Valley was explored by the Wall Street Journal reporter John Carreyrou, who exposed the Theranos scam. According to Carreyrou, "blitzscaling[21]" and the "Fake it until you make it" strategy are the main ingredients used by the region's entrepreneurs to capture the attention of private financiers and potential clients: "This means that you exaggerate your achievements and hope that reality eventually catches up with what you promised investors and the public… Steve Jobs, Larry Ellison and even Bill Gates all adopted this principle until they became successful[22]." In the IT sector, shading the truth

---

18. Bethany McLean, "'He's Full of Shit': How Elon Musk Fooled Investors, Bilked Taxpayers, and Gambled Tesla to Save SolarCity," *Vanityfair.com*, August 25, 2019.

19. *Ibid.*

20. Peter Thiel, *op. cit.*

21. The concept was created by par Reid Hoffman, a Silicon Valley investor and co-founder and executive chairman of LinkedIn: "Blitzscaling is what you do when you need to grow really, really quickly. It's the science and art of rapidly building out a company to serve a large and usually global market, with the goal of becoming the first mover at scale." Tim Sullivan, "Blitzscaling. The chaotic, sometimes grueling path to high-growth, high-impact entrepreneurship," *Harvard business Review, April 2016.*

22. John Carreyrou in an interview with Romain Gonzalez for *Le Point: Lepoint.fr*, April 19, 2019, "Theranos, la plus grande arnaque de

is commonplace, which confirms the strategy employed by Silicon Valley managers—rather than describe the value of their offer in terms of an invention or a new product, they anchor their speeches in societal aspirations, drawing a path towards a desirable future, and above all innovate in the way they tell stories, bringing collaborators and customers into their adventure. When a project is completed, its success story is celebrated in all the management manuals. But when a company loses its way, when it hits the wall of reality and crashes, the mirage fades away, revealing the extent of its deception.

The Theranos scandal is an excellent illustration of this phenomenon. Created in 2003 by Elizabeth Holmes, barely twenty years old at the time, the startup claimed it would revolutionize blood-testing with a device that could conduct hundreds of laboratory tests with just a few finger-pricks of blood. This project, which seemed to come straight out of a sci-fi movie, quickly attracted investors, and its founder grew the company to a valuation of $9 billion. Only the venture capital firm MedVenture, which specializes in the field of healthcare and medical devices, remained skeptical about this endeavor; other funds, obsessed with the "gold rush," jumped in with their eyes closed. Exploiting the myth of technological solutionism and the promise of saving thousands of lives, Elizabeth Holmes became America's new entrepreneurial icon and amassed a fortune, which led to her status as a benefactor of humanity. She contained all the elements of *junk tech*'s aspirational leadership and an unleashing of desire: "The charm offensive started [...] with Elizabeth Holmes herself (her big blue eyes, her deep voice, her strength of conviction, her almost messianic commitment). No one worried that Holmes had no established training in the highly technical disciplines used by the Theranos project. On the contrary: the fact that she had left Stanford after her first year, leading to comparisons with

---

l'histoire des startup."

such brilliant college dropouts as Steve Jobs, Bill Gates[23]" or even Mark Zuckerberg. A chink in Holmes' armor finally appeared in 2015 when John Carreyrou's investigation revealed the unreliability of its technology and its false lab practices. Theranos was actually a massive fraud.

Elizabeth Holmes built her success on a web of lies; this is undeniable. But more importantly, the company seems to have been trapped within her story and its extremely exaggerated aspirations: "Theranos seems to have started out as an honest project—crazy maybe, but honest. Then gradually, the shameful secret began to build up, simply because Theranos failed to develop the promised technology. Early attempts at calibrating it (the fake ones) were probably seen as a temporary measure: they were convinced the expected results would come soon, but they never came[24]." The startup's team failed to bridge the gap between "faking it" and "making it." Its path is symptomatic of the drifts that have multiplied in Silicon Valley in recent years[25], and shows that the boundaries between vision, "bullshit" and lies are becoming increasingly blurred[26]. Amazed by the power of *junk tech*, some entrepreneurs then suffer its adverse effects: they lose contact with reality, begin

---

23. Hervé Laroche, Christelle Théron, Véronique Steyer, "Theranos, les inavouables secrets d'une startup fraduleuse," *Theconversation.com*, September 27, 2018.

24. *Ibid.*

25. Erin Griffith, *"The Other Tech Bubble,"* *Wired.com*, December 16, 2017.

26. In the California-based magazine *Wired*, journalist Erin Griffith relates an interesting anecdote on this subject: "Even the most well-intentioned startup founders have to persuade investors, engineers, and customers to believe in a future where their totally made-up idea will be real: 'That's not 'My cola tastes better than yours.' That's 'Let me explain to you how the world's going to be,' says Chris Bulger, managing director at Bulger Partners, an investment bank that advises technology companies on acquisitions. 'Is that person lying when they turn out to be wrong?'" Erin Griffith, "Theranos and Silicon Valley's 'Fake It Till You Make It' Culture," *Wired.com*, March 14, 2018.

to live in an imaginary world and end up believing that their technology will actually change the course of history.

Investors can also fall into this trap. Take for example Masayoshi Son, the head of SoftBank and Japan's first richest man, who accumulated staggering losses after betting on some rather nutty technology. In addition to random investments in Uber and WeWork, which did not keep its promises in terms of capitalization, the businessman took some strange bets, to say the least—spending $3.4 billion to put 74 satellites in orbit "to connect the entire surface of the Earth to the Internet, from the heights of the Himalayas to the arid steppes of the North Sahara," which are now drifting in space; a grant of $400 million to the founders of "Uber for Dog Walkers," a concept that struggled to convince consumers; $240 million lost to Brandless, a San Francisco-based SME that aimed to transform the way organic products are distributed but went bankrupt in 2020, and so on[27]. Masayoshi Son's setbacks are a perfect reflection of the excess linked to *junk tech*, but they also reveal the limitations of SoftBank's strategy—by focusing on the culture of means and the prospects of high short-term added value, the Japanese group and its partners took enormous risks; they were less and less interested in the real value of the startups they were acquiring and their growth potential; they failed to see that they were betting more on existing trends (platforms less disruptive than in the early 2010s) than on future solutions.

Promising everything under the sun without technically and operationally following through leads to dead ends. While technology can sometimes be inadequate, it is absolutely necessary; without it, there is nothing left but bullshit. Marketing is a way to enhance the visibility of technology and improve our awareness of it. As Alessandro Baricco, an Italian philosopher, explains in his latest book, *The Game: A Digital Turning*

------

27. François Miguet, "Masayoshi Son ou la chute du capitalisme arrogant," *Capital.fr*, July 20, 2020.

Point, "There is no such thing as a fact without storytelling. If you are lulled by the idea that there are people in the Game who win because of their storytelling skills in a total vacuum of facts or ideas, please continue to be so. I'm not with you. The question is more subtle than you think[28]." The same goes for marketing and technology, whose relationship and interrelationship follow complex rules.

During the coronavirus crisis, we were able to look at technological solutionism with its Promethean ambitions (the idea that data, AI, the right code, algorithms, robots can solve all of mankind's problem and save us from death), and see how ridiculous it seems, how powerless it is to provide fast, concrete responses in a real emergency. We have seen classic problems anchored in a secular societal reality (a pandemic threat) dispel the mirage of Silicon Valley's dream weavers. Is it even reasonable to promise immortality, that diseases will be eradicated, that risks will be managed thanks to Big Data when a simple respiratory virus can paralyze the world economy, polarize public opinion and plunge seemingly competent healthcare systems into chaos? Doesn't the Covid-19 pandemic show that tech solutionism's goals and prospects are meaningless? With the exception of data models developed to study the transmission of the virus, AI was almost absent in managing this crisis, demonstrating (or confirming) that tech innovations had not necessarily been effective in anticipating, understanding and dealing with new, unforeseen phenomena.

Has Europe lost all ambition?

In France and Europe, we are also the victims of excess, but a completely different kind. We have lost our ability to dream and let go of our ambitions. Consumed by a kind of "indefinite

---

28. Alessandro Baricco, *The Game: A Digital Turning Point*, McSweeney's Publishing, December 2020.

pessimism[29]," we no longer seem capable of projecting ourselves into the future, of creating desirable prospects for the coming generation. With the exception of the ideal of establishing peace and stability, which remains the ultimate fiction to which the European narrative attaches itself, in what context is this project taking place? We are all free to criticize the excess of technological solutionism imported from Silicon Valley or China's approach to AI ethics. But what can France and Europe offer as compared to existing digital giants or in other parts of the world? They may have something legitimate to propose, but introducing taxes and data protection policies will never solve the major problems we are now facing, the completely different and much greater challenges that eclipse a limited defensive strategy—to develop innovation ecosystems; to restore a spirit of conquest and an appetite for taking risks; to ensure that a stronger digital Europe and French Tech are not merely slogans or platitudes but support goals that will re-enchant our vision of technology.

The challenges are complex, and we must confront the ways the European mindset has evolved since the end of the Second World War. We entered a "time of absence," as the philosopher Peter Sloterdijk[30] calls it, and abandoned the ideas of an empire, of universal influence and conquest that had been in Europe's DNA in order to transcend the circumstances. The United States and more recently China have taken up the torch and ambition to forge the future in their own image. Of course, there are objective reasons for Europe's lack of vitality. We invented and experimented with totalitarianism in the twentieth century, which made us suspicious of lofty narratives and claims of transforming the world. Broken by the conflicts of 1914-1918 and 1939-1945 and by the atrocities

---

29. Peter Thiel, *op. cit.*

30. Peter Sloterdijk, *Si l'Europe s'éveille. Réflexions sur le programme d'une puissance mondiale à la fin de l'ère de son absence politique*, Mille et une nuits, February 2003.

committed in the name of ideologies, we were narcissistically injured and lost faith in our ability to inspire the rest of the world. The myth of European conquerors and explorers was replaced by the myth of pacifists and managers ruled by the Goddess of Reason, the technocratic order, the cult of intellect and people's nostalgia for the splendor of the past—all qualities that have made the European Union a haven of tranquility and a popular tourist destination…

At the same time, Europe has not overcome the crisis that resulted from the notion of progress that were amplified in the West as of the 1970s with the first concerns about the scarcity of resources, limits to growth (the Meadows report), and the oil crisis, which would last for two decades against a backdrop of ecological disasters (Chernobyl, the Exxon Valdez oil spill) and health scandals (mad cow disease, opposition to GMOs). Haunted by risk control and skeptical of techno-scientific and industrial advances, we ended up contemplating the future as a threat. While Silicon Valley invented a credo and a cult of disruption (technological solutionism) that were instrumental in awakening new energies, Europe continued living in pessimism and disillusionment. Opinion polls clearly reflect this state of mind: nearly 70 percent of French people "think their children will live less well in tomorrow's society than they do today. And according to a survey by the Bertelsmann Foundation published in November [2018], 67 percent of Europeans believe the world 'used to be a much better place[31].'" The certainty that we will experience an irreversible decline, which also impacts the America of losers in globalization, has taken root in people's consciousness.

The switchover to digital civilization has coincided with a proliferation of technological initiatives and renewed enthusiasm; dynamic new ventures in Paris, London or Berlin are creating a sense of optimism and show that the lines are

---

31. Sylvain Besson, "La mort du progrès nous laisse vides et angoissés," *Letemps.ch*, December 27, 2018.

shifting. But for now, we remain largely dependent on Silicon Valley and its imagination. There is no European dream! The majority of our startups fail to make it to the next level or, if they do, to shine on an international scale. Although our entrepreneurs and engineers are extremely talented, we have not yet created innovation ecosystems that can compete with those in California or China. Europe is no longer considered a territory at the forefront of technological breakthroughs, either in terms of hardware or use. Reversing this trend is not just about financial means; it is a question of method and mentality. Large companies, startups, venture capital firms and European governments should develop an innovation culture that will do a better job of embracing the codes of the aspirational age.

VII.

ABANDONING MAGICAL THINKING. EUROPE PUTS ITS SKILL AND INNOVATION TO THE TEST

> "The only true voyage, the only bath in the Fountain of Youth, would be not to visit strange lands but to possess other eyes, to see the universe through the eyes of another, of a hundred others, to see the hundred universes that each of them sees, that each of them is."
>
> MARCEL PROUST,
> *The Prisoner: In Search of Lost Time*

In March 2000, in the framework of the Lisbon Strategy, the EU heads of state and government set the goal of transforming the European Union into "the most competitive and dynamic knowledge-based economy in the world, capable of sustainable economic growth with more and better jobs and greater social cohesion," and to spend at least 3 percent of each country's GDP on research. Twenty years later, we are clearly far from achieving this goal. Despite the level of scientific excellence on some university campuses and innovative clusters (Oxford, Cambridge, Munich, Paris-Saclay), Europe is in an inferior position to the United States and China: it "missed the boat [...] in terms of digital, artificial intelligence (AI) and robotics[1]," which are key drivers of the fourth industrial revolution. Public investment levels remain below the goals put forth in 2000[2]; European companies spend less money on innovation than their competitors; and venture capital firms are small compared to those in America[3]. In terms of the number of unicorn startups (those valued at or over $1 billion), Europe only has about 30, compared to 91 in China and 178 in the United States[4]. Lastly, regarding "firms well established in their market, Forbes list of the 100 top digital companies in 2018 included 49 American companies, 14 Chinese and only 12 European, of which only one was French (Dassault Systèmes) [5]."

1. Is the equation financial or cultural?

All these facts reflect the difficulty the "Old Continent" has experienced in entering the new economy on equal footing. Conscious of the threats this delay poses to the competitiveness and sovereignty of the EU states, in August 2019 many European officials called for a commission headed by Ursula von der Leyen to create a mega-fund, endowed with €100 billion, that would offer new opportunities to high-potential European

---

1. Christian Saint-Étienne, *Trump et Xi Jinping. Les apprentis sorciers*, Editions de L'Observatoire, November 2018, Marie Dancer, "Pour une Europe plus performante, un meilleur soutien à l'innovation," *La Croix*, March 25, 2019.

2. "In 2017, the European Union spent 1.96% of its GDP on research and development (R&D). China spent 2,13%, and the United States 2,79%. South Korea, Israel and Switzerland each spend between 3 and 4% of their GDP on R&D," Marie Dancer, *op. cit.*

3. *Europa.eu*, June 22, 2018, "European Innovation Scoreboard 2018: Europe must deepen its innovation edge."

4. See: www.cbinsights.com

5. Philippe Tibi, "Financer la quatrième révolution industrielle. Lever le verrou du financement des entreprises technologiques," report presented to the French Minister of Economy and Finance, July 2019.

startups, contribute to the emergence of tech giants capable of competing with GAFA, NATU and BATX, and empower Europe in such strategic sectors as cybersecurity, aerospace, AI or energy storage[6]. This initiative reflects a genuine awareness of the fact that Europe risks being left behind by Big Tech.

It would be misleading to reduce this problematic to a financial equation. Europe's main handicaps are cultural and intellectual. We have not succeeded in developing innovation ecosystems capitalizing on the achievements of our major companies, the dynamism of our startups or the talent of our researchers. Our vision is overly focused on resources and technology, which distracts us from market needs, future challenges and the aspirations of citizen-consumers. Unlike Silicon Valley, Europe has not yet tackled "its real problem, that is, how to move from fundamental discoveries, where it excels, to the commercialization of new products and services[7]." More specifically, our understanding of marketing needs to increase so that we see it not as a sales tool but as a driver to innovation!

To move in this direction, we need to do more than putting billions of euros on the table, to encourage the emergence of startups, incubators and accelerators, launching a "French Tech" label or renaming R&D directors as innovation directors… We will remain trapped in magical thinking f we focus on false priorities and a "techno-centered" approach.

In order to strengthen the culture of innovation in Europe, we believe several simple paths deserve to be explored. For large corporations and startups, the focus should be put on "marketing first" and sensitivity to emerging trends—developing disruptive technologies cannot be seen as an end in itself, and we will have taken a decisive step once we have understood that "marketing = innovation." At the same time, governments

---

6. Sylvain Rolland, "Vers un méga-fonds européen de 100 milliards d'euros pour créer des champions de la tech?," *Latribune.fr*, August 26, 2019.

7. Marie Dancer, *op. cit.*

would benefit from building on the DARPA Model for Transformative Technologies, laying the foundations for an ecosystem that takes on the societal challenges we will face in the future. Although these ingredients have been key to the success of agents of *junk tech*, we should not try to copy the Silicon Valley recipe. This would be undesirable, because hardware and deep tech would take on as much importance as software[8]. This would doubtless not be feasible as we move towards an increasingly regulated world in which innovations will have to bear in mind account the tightening of existing legislation and citizens' aspirations to use tech solutions that are more virtuous and address society's most pressing challenges.

Just as the junk food industry has had to adapt to new consumer desires and to the government's increasing focus on healthier eating, *junk tech* will probably have to adjust its model in order to survive. While Californian startups prospered in the 1990s and 2000s in a comparative legal vacuum and within a system of relative "permissionlessness[9]," everything today seems to indicate that the technologies of the 2020s will be disseminated in a much more restrictive, more normative global framework.

---

8. This is one of the hypotheses put forth by Peter Thiel, one of stagnation: "Innovation in the past forty years has been too confined to a narrow domain: computers, information technology, Internet, mobile Internet in the world of bits. But nothing really new in the world of hardware, health, biotech, clean and inexpensive energy, space travel, underwater cities." Dominique Nora, "Peter Thiel, le techno-prophète accueilli comme une rock-star en France," *Nouvelobs.com*, February 28, 2016.

9. Adam D. Thierer, "Embracing a Culture of Permissionless Innovation," *Cato.org*, November 17, 2014.

2. "MARKETING FIRST" VS. DISRUPTION AT ALL COSTS

Open innovation and magical thinking in startups

The insufficient attention paid to marketing and the damage done by magical thinking are reflected in the recurring failure of open innovation strategies, an approach that borrows precepts from Silicon Valley. Around 90 percent of companies think they innovate too slowly, and some 80 to 90 percent of innovation centers fail and end up wasting resources. These two figures, highlighted a few years ago by Altimeter and Capgemini Consulting[10], summarize the paradoxical difficulty experienced by many large companies: the want open innovation, but the results are rarely commensurate with the efforts made[11].

This discrepancy is the result of a phenomenon typical of the digital civilization and its trends: open innovation is constrained by magical thinking in startups. Traditional companies think of startups in a way that is idealized, distorted or deficient. They consider themselves insufficiently innovative, because they are cut off from the creative thinkers and misfits dear to Steve Jobs, who use the "first principles thinking" Elon Musk talks about, without being subject to the constraints and obstacles of a pyramid organizational structure. Most of the time, the goal of an open innovation strategy is to identify startups and invite them to partner with large companies in order to drive innovation by drawing on the startups' vitality, on their newer ideas and working methods. However, these collaborations often remain frustrating because traditional companies are not necessarily suited to listening to

---

10. *Capgemini.com*, July 23, 2015, "Capgemini Consulting and Altimeter global report reveals leading businesses continue to struggle with innovation, with traditional R&D model 'broken.'"

11.. Jean-Marc Bally, "Pourquoi l'open innovation ne marche pas pour les grandes entreprises," *Latribune.fr*, November 3, 2016.

partner or integrated startups. In addition, as venture capitalists know, the reality of startups is sometimes disappointing:
98 percent of them fail because they are unable to identify and
develop business models capable of understanding or transforming a market. They are doomed to make ends meet, face
bankruptcy or be resold under conditions that fall far below
their original financial expectations. When these startups do
manage to convince one or more investors to participate in
their development project, the numbers improve, but this is
far from a guarantee of success: fewer than 20 percent of the
resulting companies are considered remarkable investments
and lead to the radical transformation of a market. Disruption
happens rarely[12].

Faced with the hundreds of thousands of euros raised
by the majority of startups, large companies devote billions
of euros to R&D and have resources that are often unique,
experienced people and a capacity for innovation that is organized and massive, but they have not yet found the recipe for
major advances. They see every startup as a giant killer, which
says a great deal about some companies' defensive posture…
In reality, Uber not only did not eliminate taxi operators but
was itself challenged by other startups; Airbnb did not destroy
Accor[13], nor did LendingClub cause Wells Fargo to disappear.
The primary ambition of these newcomers was not necessarily
to put an end to their historic competitors; they just wanted
to appropriate or transform part of the market.

---

12. *Ibid.*

13. Big business in France threatened by uberization have proven it
can react and resist the pure play tech companies by developing its offer
and conducting digital transformation from a marketing point of view
without giving up fundamentals. There is no need to be "disruptive" in
all circumstances!

From inspiration to aspiration

Our intention is not to belittle startups; on the contrary, they are incredible structures, full of talent, energy and enthusiasm that make a real difference. But to successfully create an open innovation culture, large companies should not necessarily consider individual startups—interacting with a cohort of startups is the key to transforming markets, revealing trends and understanding customers' aspirations. Startups are driven by ambition and commitment that spring from a combination of entrepreneurial drive and "strategic thinking" that generally corresponds to an unprecedented contextualization of market experience and a keen observation of emerging opportunities. They bring a new perspective. For this reason, large companies that want to be truly innovative should adopt an approach similar to that of venture capital investors, but adapting it to the environment and the challenges of a traditional group: identifying weak signals, analyzing the ecosystem of emerging players and anticipating developments in the value chain that could represent significant potential for transformation in the years to come.

In short, you need to fight for the right outcome—while working with a few young innovative companies is certainly useful, it reinforces a belief in the structural incapacity of large companies to be innovative. The first goal of an open innovation strategy is to understand the value chains and their potential for change, to examine and confront the swarms of startups around you, to identify potential disruptions and reconfigurations in your sector that can become either threats or opportunities. It is first and foremost a question of marketing[14]!

Innovating is also results from curiosity and openness. You need to immerse yourself in your environment, associate with peers, observe how other companies operate and not

---

14.. *Ibid.*

hesitate to share ideas or initiatives. Rather than inventing by any means necessary, it is preferable to look within your ecosystem for sources of inspiration to help determine or anticipate your clients' aspirations. The French entrepreneur Jean-Baptiste Rudelle describes Silicon Valley's corporate culture as an approach based on trust, mutual helpfulness and the ability to organize itself in terms of networks: "The Valley has a participatory culture that is unique in the world. It is the antithesis of the autocratic culture that dominates the world of SMEs. And it is this culture that has given rise to startups in their current form. Some trace this back to the conquest of the West. At the time, crossing the United States was a long and dangerous journey. Pioneers had to deal with many unforeseen situations and adapt as best they could. [...] One of the keys to survival was to join forces with other pioneers to form convoys that followed the same route together[15]." Developing innovation ecosystems implies strengthening this culture of collaboration and exchange[16]. Our startups and large companies have every interest in working together—not just in order to defend French Tech or European Tech, but to refine their knowledge of markets, rely on collective intelligence[17], facilitate risk-taking and accelerate their economic growth.

---

15. Jean-Baptiste Rudelle, *op. cit.*

16. "The idea of the ecosystem refers [...] to the efficiency of decentralized, open structures composed of a wide variety of actors in constant interaction, which develops thanks to a permanent mix of competition and cooperation." Pierre Veltz, *La société hyper-industrielle. Le nouveau capitalisme productif,* Seuil, February 2017.

17. Émile Servan-Schreiber, *Supercollectif. La nouvelle puissance de nos intelligences,* Fayard, October 2018.

3. What are the innovations in our future?

Towards a European DARPA?

The European public authorities can obviously give an impetus to this movement. As seen with the Defense Advanced Research Projects Agency (DARPA), which is at the origin of many technologies that have been beneficial for California companies[18], strategic targeting of innovation support has positive effects on the ecosystem in place. For Europe, it is no longer time to look in the rear-view mirror, dwell on missed opportunities or try to catch up in areas where the battle is already lost. We are not going to create another Google, Facebook or Apple. It's time to take on future challenges where nothing is yet decided, especially in the world of hardware, deep tech and infrastructure. Optimizing immature technologies and opening up unknown horizons to meet future societal challenges would be the best ways to build a Europe of innovation and re-engage with the aspirational age.

As advocated by the Joint European Disruptive Initiative (JEDI), which is calling for the creation of an equivalent to DARPA, it is essential to change methods and software in terms of innovation. Since the beginning of 2010, the European Commission has spent more than €70 billion on research, or about €10 billion per year, without this coinciding with a technological leap of "the Old Continent"—an amount far greater than DARPA's annual budget of around $3 billion[19]. The question is not money, but how to use these funds and how to conduct the innovation projects of rupture: "In addition to the 50 million euros, European rules require 9 countries and 20 participants to be on board. People spend more time

———————————

18. For more information on this, see Chapter II.

19. Solène Davesne, "Chercheurs, startup, innovateurs, soyez prêts : le réveil du JEDI, c'est pour septembre," *Usinenouvelle.com*, August 24, 2018.

coordinating than doing research[20]." To gain speed and agility, JEDI plans to launch challenges subsidized for about €10 million, and to select the most innovative projects in a few weeks, putting startups, research centers and large groups on an equal footing.

These challenges will focus on structural issues related to the future of mobility, health, energy, agriculture and telecommunications, with, for example "the development of a more energy-efficient blockchain, the creation of quantum links with satellites, which would make them more competitive with 5G [...], the replacement of glyphosate or the recovery of space debris in low orbit, which is essential to continue to exploit the potential of space[21]." Modelled on DARPA's methodology, which pits different players against each other to compete for futuristic ambitions, JEDI also aims to decompartmentalize public and private research and build more bridges between the worlds of inventors and innovators. It is an interesting mechanism for encouraging projects that are extremely risky to finance, creating a breeding ground for breakthrough innovations, tackling projects that make sense for citizen-consumers in the twenty-first century (energy transition, climate change, pollution control, smart cities, etc.) and setting the technological standards for future industry. European technology should inspire dreams and enthusiasm.

In other words, such an initiative will be successful if and only if it cultivates the aspirational dimension and sets exciting goals that seem unattainable at first glance. Betting on deep tech, hardware or future infrastrucures is only worthwhile if it focuses on the uses that will result from it. We need to ask ourselves how technologies in the twenty-first century will profoundly improve people's daily lives, above and beyond narcissistic dynamics, and positively transform societies. More than ever, Europe must position itself in this niche to offer

---

20. *Ibid.*
21. *Ibid.*

an alternative to California's *junk tech* and put its innovative potential at the service of a certain vision of the common good—for example, the advent of "zero defects" models and removal of "plastic from the continent," construction of the first Smart City with a human face, total decarbonization of the economy and responses to the climate emergency, discovery of habitable planets outside the solar system. These are all challenges that can reawaken our technological power and generate a collective momentum. It is on these new foundations that governments and financial institutions must orient their funding, focusing on expanding their marketing efforts for the most promising technologies.

To achieve this, Europeans would win by capitalizing on their industrial strengths and promoting cross-sectoral cooperation (such as automotive and telecommunications) in order to tackle future innovation projects head on[22]. Leading the battle in the field of standards—as was once the case with GSM—and data would also be desirable to transform the manna of available data into a lever for economic growth. This could involve opening up government and anonymized data in strategic sectors (urban transport, health, etc.) in order to encourage the emergence of services in high-potential market segments[23]. At the same time, it would be important to raise citizens' awareness of the use, control and dissemination of their personal data[24] in order to strengthen transparency and individual responsibility and to involve users in the development of businesses that respect their privacy, free will and expectations.

---

22. McKinsey Global Institute, *Innovation in Europe. Changing the game to regain a competitive edge*, October 2019.
23. *Ibid.*
24. *Ibid.*

The 2020s: a world of restricted innovation?

Imitating the Americans and Silicon Valley in every respect would not, in fact, be a good idea. Today, we are likely coming to the end of a cycle marked by the triumph of software companies and *junk tech* in a context of favorable regulations in which their novelty worked in their favor. In the United States, the digital revolution was stimulated during the 1990s by the Telecommunications Act of 1996, which notably avoided regulating the Internet in a manner as rigid as that applied to earlier communications and media technologies. In addition, a Tax Freedom Act was passed in 1998 to block governments from imposing discriminatory taxes on digital, e-commerce and platform-related businesses. These decisions encouraged "permissionless innovation" which, combined with the freedom to experiment, led to an outpouring of innovations that allowed startups to develop at high speed and become digital giants[25]. As for their expansion into Europe, it has been facilitated by the legal loopholes surrounding these business models and the absence of regulatory and fiscal harmonization across the continent. Until recently, Silicon Valley's "dealers" enjoyed relative impunity.

At this stage, only China prevented GAFA and NATU from entering the country in order to stimulate the emergence of its own superstars, BATX. As Niall Ferguson, a Scottish historian, explains in his most recent book *The Square and the Tower*, Americans misdiagnosed the Chinese authorities' reaction. They long imagined that the Chinese would adopt a purely defensive posture in trying to control the Internet, a method that Bill Clinton said was "trying to nail Jell-O [the wiggly gelatin dessert] to the wall[26]." But China has gone much further than the United States anticipated at the turn

---

25. Adam D. Thierer, *op. cit.*

26.. Niall Ferguson, *The Square and the Tower.* Networks and Power, from the Freemasons to Facebook, Penguin Press, January 2018.

of the twentieth century: "Yet censorship is not the key to the Chinese response to the networked age. The core of the strategy has been, by fair means and foul, to limit the access of the big American IT companies to the Chinese market and to encourage local entrepreneurs to build a Chinese answer to FANG" (Facebook, Amazon, Netflix, Google), which led to the blocking of access to Facebook in 2009, the departure of Google in 2010 and the partial withdrawal of Uber in 2016 with a deal to sell Chinese operations to its rival, Didi Chuxing, the leading vehicle for hire platform[27]. In a world where commercial wars are raging more than ever, Donald Trump's America was not to be outdone: after Huawei was banned from using Google's Android license for its smartphones, the U.S. administration in turn threatened the TikTok platform with restrictions in the summer of 2020. For digital actors who until now have enjoyed relative freedom in Western countries, these inter-state rivalries make the situation even more complex. By pointing out the flaws and dangers of technologies imported from the Middle Kingdom, the Americans did their utmost to ensure that made in China is as less aspirational as possible.

In an effort to protect their economic interests, the Chinese have used regulation and control of the digital ecosystem to consolidate existing power and expand surveillance of citizens through state-linked companies that collect massive amounts of data on individuals. With services directly inspired by *junk tech*'s flagship products—such as WeChat, owned by the Tencent group, a messaging application similar to Facebook and WhatsApp—addiction becomes a mechanism for coercion[28]. The promoters of *Big Brother made in China* under-

---

27. Uber's decision was "the result of Didi's great agility and greater financial resources as well as regulatory changes designed to give Uber difficulty in the Chinese market." *Ibid.*

28. "WeChat is used by 86% of Chinese Internet users and is rapidly replacing the business card, once mandatory in China, with QR codes that are easy to activate." *Ibid.*

stood that addiction to digital devices was a highly effective weapon to distract citizens and strengthen the grip of the dictatorship. For them, as for Californians, the key factor in the equation is less the 'tech' aspect than the 'junk' aspect.

In short, the rise of BATX was an unexpected scenario that turned things upside down and contributed to the birth of three blocs in the digital civilization: Silicon Valley, which innovates: China, which imitates; and Europe, which regulates, especially in AI and data protection. What is equally surprising in the early 2020s is that the United States and more specifically California are beginning to shift gears in terms of regulations. Under public pressure, the excess of *junk tech* is becoming less and less tolerated—in June 2019, the increase in the number of vapes among teenagers and Juul's "aggressive marketing campaign[29]" led to the banning of e-cigarettes in San Francisco; in September 2019, complaints by Uber and Lyft drivers about their working conditions and violations of labor laws led to the injunction by a California judge to classify them as employees; at the same time, more and more voices are calling for the dismantling of GAFA and antitrust investigations are multiplying; with the election of Donald Trump, "the digital industry has been accused of all evils: misuse of personal data (the Cambridge Analytica scandal), content moderation that is too strict or on the contrary too lax, anti-competitive practices… […]. The United States, until now much less severe than Europe on these various subjects, turned against its champions. Senators and House Representatives are working on laws on moderation and data protection. 'Suddenly, Silicon Valley, until now the darling of American industry, has become the big villain[30].'" Of course,

---

29. Corine Lesnes, "San Francisco interdit la vente de cigarettes électroniques pour restreindre le vapotage chez les jeunes," *Lemonde.fr*, June 26, 2019.

30. Lucie Ronfaut, "La crise de foi des employés de la Silicon Valley," *Lefigaro.fr*, September 16, 2019.

it is too early to say whether this movement will curb the innovative capacity of Californian companies and coincide with a decline in their global hegemony.

What is certain, though, is that starting with their conception, future innovations will have to take into account the growing tendency of Western companies to frame new technologies and to conform to their ethics. There will undoubtedly be a conflict in values between the aspiration to enjoy freedom and narcissism and the desire to limit the perverse effects of these innovations (polarization of the labor market, negative externalities linked to the explosion of physical and digital flows, digital addiction, loss of free will, etc.). This steep path can be an opportunity for Europe if it abandons the magical thinking of its genius inventors and draws lessons from a world in which "junk" is more important than "tech." The mechanisms that create product addicts should also be exploited in order to serve virtuous technologies, especially at a time when the Covid-19 health crisis is partly reshuffling the cards.

Instead of hiding behind regulations as if they were an embattled fortress, Europe should use these tools to trace the contours of a digital humanism that reconciles people's deepest desires with the future balance of our societies. One of the challenges facing European entrepreneurs is to take up this mission—which might seem impossible—to capture the essence of marketing and to identify the unprecedented aspirations of a century in which the triumph of Narcissus may not be history's ultimate horizon.

To put this into a clearer context, people need to realize that the coronavirus is actually offering Europe many new opportunities. We will indeed witness a kind of reboot with a transformation of usage; the Californians will have to invent other recipes. To a certain extent, in Europe we are starting from scratch, and we are going to see the emergence of an ecosystem in which European values and positioning can work in our favor: from data protection to ecological concern, from responsible agriculture to the regeneration of healthcare systems that are at the heart of their social model, the inhabitants of the "Old Continent" have a real card to play.

The €750 billion recovery plan put in place by the European Union in the summer of 2020 provides an excellent opportunity for this. In France, for instance, the recovery plan relies on three pillars that will put this financial manna to excellent use: green transition; innovation and competitiveness; and social and territorial cohesion. Investing intelligently in these areas for the next ten years will not only respond to the economic impact of the health crisis and avoid a recession, it will also maintain France among the most competitive countries in areas that are key for the nation's technological and industrial future. France must not miss the opportunity to reposition itself at the forefront of innovation!

Conclusion

Preventing an Overdose: The Search for Authenticity

> "All excess is based on man's desire to relive pleasure beyond the limits ordinarily imposed by nature. The less the human spirit is occupied, the more it tends towards excess; the mind is irresistibly drawn to it. [...] It transpires that the more societies are civilised and at peace, the more they indulge in excess."
>
> Honoré de Balzac,
> *Treatise on Modern Stimulants*

In an article published in February 2019, Tim O'Reilly—an entrepreneur known to the general public for popularizing the term Web 2.0—warned against the blitzscaling strategy promoted by Reid Hoffman and Chris Yeh[1]. According to O'Reilly, this approach partially worked for GAFA because it funded business models and innovations that profoundly

---

1. For more information on this, see Chapter VI. Reid Hoffman, Chris Yeh, *Blitzscaling. The Lightning-Fast Path to Building Massively Valuable Companies, Currency*, October 2018.

revolutionized their markets and anticipated changes their competition hadn't even identified yet [2]. In addition, the growth of these multinationals was not the result of massive spending to help amass new clients; all of them achieved profitability (Google, Apple, Facebook) or positive cash flow (Amazon) before going public.

Unlike today's platforms, which spend huge amounts of money to attract users and take advantage of network effects—without necessarily breaking even—the first generation of 2.0 companies was built on a very solid foundation. Just one fact is enough to show the difference between GAFA and their younger counterparts: over a single year, Uber squandered "more money than Amazon's accumulated losses of $3 billion from 1995 to 2002[3]," and there is nothing to indicate that this will not be the case again in 2020. In addition, these new companies are coming under increasing criticism in the United States: accused of pushing their development at their stakeholders' expense (workers, suppliers) and of damaging the social environment[4], they have lost the status they enjoyed a few years ago.

1. Is there a cast shadow over Silicon Valley?

It seems as if these companies abandoned the famous Google mantra "Don't be evil[5]," preferring instead the kind of "Winner takes all" logic that moves them away from the

---

2. For Tim O'Reilly, "Venture-backed blitzscaling was far less important to their success than product and business-model innovation, brilliant execution, and relentless strategic focus. Hypergrowth was the *result* rather than the *cause* of these companies' success." Tim O'Reilly, "The fundamental problem with Silicon Valley's favorite growth strategy," *Qz.com*, February 5, 2019.

3. Christophe Alix, "Dans la Silicon Valley, les 'licornes' font des bulles," *Liberation.fr*, May 9, 2019.

4. Tim O'Reilly, *op. cit.*

5.. This slogan has since been replaced by the motto "*Do the right thing.*"

market's fundamental values. They no longer embody the forces of good. Silicon Valley's image and seductive narrative have been somewhat damaged. Most of them have not grabbed onto the aspirations emerging in Europe and across the Atlantic: customers and employees have higher expectations of private industry, and in the "era of social consciousness,[6]" they expect companies to have values, to stand for something, to work for the common good in one way or another. For example, 70 percent of Americans believe companies should take action on issues that aren't directly relevant to their core business; two-thirds believe that corporate leaders should initiate positive policy changes instead of government[7]. Seen from this perspective, it is not surprising that the champions of *junk tech* are under attack—their services are seen as less and less valuable to people and society.

More generally, Silicon Valley's funding model raises questions. Although it may have been adapted to innovations in the 1990s and 2000s, in the context of the boom in the software industry and the rapid growth of information and communication technology, will it conform to future innovations? Many experts are doubtful, and assert that startups specialized in hardware, deep tech and industrial technologies are having a hard time finding their place in the Californian ecosystem[8]… in contrast to projects with more questionable goals (Juicero, Theranos, WeWork), which over time have tended to multiply.

These misgivings do not mean that Silicon Valley is dead; it still has a clear lead over Europe. But they do pose questions about its future and on the longevity of *junk tech*. By radicalizing the precepts that were critical to its success, and by

---

6. Larry Weber, *Authentic Marketing. How to Capture Hearts and Minds Through the Power of Purpose*, Wiley, January 2019.

7. *Ibid.*

8. Greg Satell, "Why Some of the Most Groundbreaking Technologies Are a Bad Fit for the Silicon Valley Funding Model," *Hbr.org*, April 5, 2018.

injecting forever greater amounts of capital into their unicorns to boost their performance or finance innovative gadgets, isn't Silicon Valley on the verge of overdosing? Everything seems to suggest that these Californians have become victims of their own myths, and of the perils of technological solutionism.

This theory cannot be ruled out in so far as the most respected ambassadors of *junk tech* seem trapped, forever rushing to move forward, as if they were more and more detached, more and more in a bubble—Elon Musk making a series of announcements so surprising that many observers became skeptical; Uber pushing its self-driving car in order to prove its profitability; WeWork, the self-described "real-estate-as-a-service," showcasing its trove of big data in determining "the optimal size of a conference room or the best number of coffee machines to install,[9]" without clearly demonstrating the concrete use of tech and innovation in its business model. Although the cash machine continues spitting out money for Silicon Valley's flagship companies, certain mechanisms are beginning to stall.

2. AUTHENTIC MARKETING: AN ALTERNATIVE TO THE EXCESSES OF *JUNK TECH*?

The French and Europeans have all the necessary assets to build a credible alternative to this marketing model, and conserving only the best parts: the power of innovation based on marketing and the dynamics of creating product addiction. These dynamics can be used to achieve virtuous goals, just as narcissism can be a driving force in areas such as responsible consumption, sustainable agriculture or the reduction of carbon emissions[10]. Consumers' aspirations to live in a world

---

9. Vincent Fagot, "WeWork, entreprise technologique en toc?" *Lemonde. fr*, August 31, 2019.

10. For more information on this, see Chapter III. Thanks to the work Richard Thaler, winner of the Nobel Prize in economics, and Carl Sunstein,

that is less polluted, less one-sided and less dehumanized can become a driving force for startups and companies that generate technological and industrial solutions for these goals.

This is all about putting marketing—in the noblest sense of the word—at the center of their value proposition, which means tapping into the zeitgeist, finding a higher purpose, building a coherent offer, reducing complexity, shaping narratives that resonate with personal and collective desires. In this respect, it is not enough to claim that you will "elevate the world's consciousness," as WeWork founder Adam Neumann grandly (or cynically) announced. You also need to match words with deeds by moving from story*telling* to story *making*. French and European companies would have every interest in prioritizing authentic marketing to prove that they are no longer "moving [their] organization from telling stories to actually being an active part of them. [...] to impact a problem, to make the world a better place.[11]". With the existence of so many worthwhile projects—from the fight against global warming to the infrastructure of Smart Cities, from new mobility needs to energy transition—a host of innovations can still be imagined in order to give the future a more desirable face.

There is no need to develop revolutionary processes to achieve this goal and reposition yourself in the global competition. Authenticity is a form of sobriety in front of the flashy hues of the technology mirage. The history of innovation reveals that making strategic and relevant adjustments to one's offer has given rise to the world's greatest successes. At the dawn of the consumer society, for example, Henry Ford—wrongly attributed with the invention of the automobile—took

---

a legal scholar, we know that "choice architecture" can be used to encourage individuals to adopt better behaviors without restricting freedom of choice (known as the nudge theory). In the same way, narcissism and the desire to contribute to the common good can benefit companies that give their customers the feeling they are working together in this sense.

11. Larry Weber, *op. cit.*

existing technologies (car manufacturing, the assembly line) and perfected them to create a product accessible to the greatest number of people[12]. This lesson is still valid in the aspirational age. We need above all to be attentive to emerging trends and changing mindsets in order to transform market segments. With a million startups, including 15,000 in France[13], the sources of inspiration for developing a forward-looking vision are at our fingertips.

To bank on authentic marketing ultimately means renouncing the excess and artifice of *junk tech* and returning to the essence of innovation: the ability to respond to our highest aspirations. The Covid-19 crisis has made this observation even more significant. What has happened—and is still happening—is destabilizing people's habits and behavior. In the space of barely six months, so many people were confronted with the same problems (fear of the virus, the constraints of lockdown, the development of teleworking, recourse to new forms of mobility, the need to privilege local consumption, etc.). Many people have begun changing their lives, and many have seen their daily ways of functioning disrupted. This evolution represents an incredible opportunity, a fertile breeding ground for successful marketing. In a context in which change is ubiquitous, even more things can be invented. The challenge facing France and Europe is to convert this period of uncertainty into a powerful transformational vector.

3. NARCISSUS AND THE MIRROR OF THE WORLD

Since the Second World War, we have moved from the mass market to mass individualism to mass narcissism. While lower prices and overconsumption were principal motivators in the old world, we have gradually shifted to a world in which

---

12. *Ibid.*
13. Source: Aster Fab.

people want to be better consumers, in which marketing and hyper-segmentation are becoming more and more present. In the past, technological superiority was the market's main driving force. Today it is a necessary ingredient, but it is not sufficient for reaching our goals. The quest for meaning is becoming increasingly important, as is the addictive nature of products and services that increasingly resonate with the personal and collective unconscious.

The paradox of our age is that Narcissus is gradually integrating the world into his ego. Narcissus is aware that he can no longer act alone—that the future of the planet depends on some kind of altruism. One of the biggest challenges facing existing and future companies is to accompany this goal, to imagine solutions and a purpose that incorporates brand altruism, however incongruous that may seem. In the future, the transformation of sectors and technologies needs to serve the environment, to bring interest convergence to a global community on such varied subjects as reducing carbon emissions, pollution, health care and strategies for a circular economy.

Narcissistic individuals are beginning to perceive the negative character of the repetitiveness (addiction to social networks and digital devices, the logic of over-consumption, the infinite quest for recognition, wasted resources) and stagnation created by *junk tech*. It is vital is for those creating new technologies to help people and companies manage this situation by transforming product addiction into a positive vehicle for change. From now on, marketing should respond to consumer behavior with products and services that are beneficial for society and the planet. They should eschew Narcissus' dark side and focusing instead on his reflection—a reflection that is more flattering, that no longer looks to others for approval and admiration, that prefers instead to do good, to beautify and magnify the world—thus transforming the world into a mirror of the self in order to serve altruism.

Contents